From

Public School
TO THE
Ivy League

How to get into a top school
without top dollar resources

MANDEE HELLER ADLER
WITH AIMEE HELLER

FIRST EDITION

BIOGRAPHICAL PUBLISHING COMPANY
PROSPECT, CONNECTICUT

From Public School to the Ivy League
How to get into a top school without top dollar resources
First Edition

PUBLISHED BY:
Biographical Publishing Company
95 Sycamore Drive
Prospect, CT 06712-1493
Phone: 203-758-3661
Fax: 253-793-2618
e-mail: biopub@aol.com

Copyright © Mandee Heller Adler, Aimee Heller
Edited by: Cheree Heller Liebowitz
Cover designed by: Michael Quanci
Cover photo copyright ©: Steven Minicola, University of Pennsylvania
Back cover photo copyright ©: Andy Ale for DP3 Studio

Fourth Printing 2014
PRINTED IN THE UNITED STATES OF AMERICA

Publisher's Cataloging-in-Publication Data
Adler, Mandee Heller; Heller, Aimee
From Public School to the Ivy League : How to get into a top school without top dollar resources/ by Mandee Heller Adler and Aimee Heller.– 1st ed.
p. cm.
ISBN 1-929882-92-0
13 Digit ISBN 9781929882922
1. Title. 2. College guides. 3. Ivy League schools. 4. College entrance.
5. Career guidance. 6. Higher education.
BISAC CODES:
      STU010000 STUDY AIDS / College Guides
      STU009000 STUDY AIDS / College Entrance
      EDU031000 EDUCATION / Counseling / Career Guidance
Dewey Decimal Classification: 378 Higher Education
Library of Congress Control Number: 2013946174

Table of Contents

Prologue

I was one of two students in a class of 550+ who went to an Ivy League school from a terrific public school in Miami Beach, FL. It wasn't that other students didn't want to, or didn't deserve to. They were presidents of clubs; captains of teams; nationally ranked in science, music, or debate; in the top ten of our class; or had a combination of many achievements. But the Ivies said no. It just fit the pattern. For many years at my school, less than a handful of kids would go to the Ivy League, even though many, who deserved to go, applied.

While I was obviously thrilled for my own accomplishment— acceptance to the University of Pennsylvania—I was surprised by the disproportionate number of acceptances that went to students at our neighboring private school. While only two students received Ivy acceptances from my high school, ten students got accepted to Penn alone from the smaller private school! When I went to college, I remember wondering why many of those students were there, especially on the nights I was tutoring them in subjects like economics.

Clearly, these students came from higher-income families, but I was fairly certain that didn't really correspond to higher intellect.

The private school kids had it different. They had to have it different. But what was the real difference that made a difference? They didn't score higher on the AP tests or have pre-knowledge of the SAT. We took the same classes as the private school students (in some cases, we took even more APs), and we received the same accolades in national academic competitions. Why did it seem that our fellow public school students didn't get past the Ivy admissions gate?

What did these students have that my classmates did not? What did they know that we did not?

I was determined to figure it out. I gathered the data, analyzed it, and even met with the superintendent of the Miami-Dade Public School system and other education experts.

My interest in college admissions eventually landed me in the CEO seat: running a global college counseling business that helps students from all over the world find and get into colleges and graduate schools. Of course, working in college counseling, I've heard all kinds of rumors about college admissions. From the highly doubtful: "My friend's cousin got accepted to Harvard with a 3.0 GPA due to a fabulous essay," to the factually incorrect: "the SAT starts to average the scores after three times."

But, another claim I often hear is that students from private schools have a more difficult curriculum, are "better" students, and therefore deserve to get into better colleges. And, while there is possibly a disproportionate number of private school students in top schools, I do not believe the quality of private school curricula or student body to be the primary reasons for such acceptance rates.

What made their chances of getting into an Ivy League school higher? After much travel and thought, a conclusion was drawn:

The private school students enjoyed a much higher counselor-per-student ratio.

In other words, they were informed—and informed early—about the college admissions process.

At our public high school, there was no one who was actively engaged in getting us into a college on a personal level. There was no one to tell us what kind of topic to choose for our essay, what classes would best position us for admissions, or even how to list our extra-curriculars to our advantage. With one college counselor for a school of over 2,500 students, in retrospect, this is hardly surprising. Of course, it's hard to fault the public schools for this. Public schools have to accept all the students and problems that private schools won't take, while also worrying about the constant threat and reality of budget cuts. Children who were already succeeding and wanted to reap the highest fruits of success—they weren't always a priority.

The students at private schools often have very strong college counseling offices. The very best counselors know each student personally. They help students choose colleges and prepare the applications as individuals. The simple attention given to the students can make the difference between admissions and rejection. Just knowing what to do can make a huge difference.

Private school students had insight into the admissions process that we didn't have.

You can't change the system, but you can change your approach. Reading this book is a great start. And of course, for hands-on support, consider an independent college counselor, such as one from the company that I run: International College Counselors.

Getting into the school of your dreams comes not from wealth, but from understanding the admissions process and committing yourself to maximizing your academic and extracurricular opportunities. As with most things, knowledge is power.

This book is that equalizer. You can still succeed and get into the school of your dreams without the private school tuition!

Three sisters who all went from a title one public school to their first-choice college created this book. I set my heart early on an Ivy League, and the others didn't want to. My oldest sister, who helped write this book, went to Boston University, a top school in the country for advertising, which was her dream career. She became a copywriter, then a creative director at a major New York advertising agency, and her writing helped make this possible. My youngest sister, a nationally ranked athlete, was co-founder and captain of the University of Florida's women's water polo team and in the Honors Program. For anyone who knows water polo and academics, that's no joke. She took her competitive drive to find the publisher and help with the editing. It was a family affair, as have been all my greatest achievements to date.

Of course, the three of us alone is only part of the story: To Jason Adler, Rebecca Adler, Sara Pearl Adler, Beverly Buxbaum Heller, David Heller, Penelope Rose Heller, Barry Liebowitz, David Liebowitz, and Matthew Liebowitz, we love you!

Chapter 1:

Admissions Overview: What Colleges Look For

WHAT COLLEGE ADMISSIONS OFFICERS WANT

"Pick me!" "Pick me!" your application says to a college.

But, what exactly are colleges looking for?

Colleges have many students to consider, especially since they're getting more and more applications each year. More students are looking to attend college, and applications like the Common Application have made it much easier for students to apply to more schools.

Back in my day, you'd have to fill out each college application. By hand. In pen. Or align it perfectly into a typewriter. You'd have to type the essay on a typewriter. If you made a mistake, you'd be typing it all over again. And you'd have to write and type a whole new essay for each school. But it's a whole new ballgame now.

For college admissions officers, the Common Application and others like it mean they have more work to do. Of course, like all people, they look to make the work easier for themselves.

They've accomplished this by coming up with easy ways to cut applicants. Did you try to beat the system? Snip. Did you plagiarize your essay? Snip. Did you embarrass yourself big time on social media? Snip. Did you try to make high school easier on yourself by taking less rigorous classes? Snip. Snip. Snip.

Then they've come up with a formula of sorts for the rest. Keep in mind that each school is different. This is a generic guideline.

THE ADMISSIONS HIERARCHY

Strength of Curriculum, a.k.a. High School Courses: Supreme Importance

The majority of admissions officers consistently place the greatest weight on the strength of a student's high school curriculum in the decision-making process. Colleges notice whether you took the most rigorous classes available to you or whether you opted for an easier route.

Grades in the Challenging Courses: Supreme Importance Runner-Up

Colleges prefer you take challenging courses. It's better to challenge yourself and risk getting a "B" than go for an easy "A." However, don't take a class that will sink you. If you take Advanced Placement (AP) calculus and get a "C," it may not be as good as an "A" in a slightly easier class. Slightly easier does not mean laughably easy.

I recommend you take high school classes one level above your comfort level.

Standardized Test Scores: High Importance

SAT scores and ACT scores usually rank third. The SAT scores are often judged in "score bands," especially when combined with a top transcript. So, for example, an Ivy League school may consider a combined mathematics and critical reading score of 1400–1600 a "score band." If you score below 1400, you are in a different category, but anywhere within the 1400–1600 score band is considered a strong score. The same is true for an ACT score, where a strong score range is 33–36.

This means you shouldn't stress about getting 10 more SAT points. If you've scored well, you're done. Turn your attention to your grades instead.

HOWEVER, students who want high scholarships need higher scores.

Students looking for special programs, like engineering, need to make sure their math scores are as high as possible.

College Essay: High Importance for "Maybes," Medium Importance for All Others

Decent essays will not get you into school or keep you out of it, EXCEPT if you're in the "maybe" pile. Of course, you won't know if you're in the maybe pile, so I recommend you do your absolute best on the essays. Finish them over the summer so you have maximum time to get them perfect.

College Fit: High Importance

Show a college you belong there and want to be there by doing your homework and sharing your knowledge in essays and interviews. If a college asks for an "optional" essay to go along with the Common App or their regular application, "optional" means "mandatory."

Extracurricular Activities: High Importance

Extracurricular activities are those activities you perform outside your normal high school curriculum. These activities may include athletics, creative arts, student government, speech and debate, internships, community service, and so much more. Colleges love students with diverse interests and goals. Keep in mind that whatever activity you participate in, colleges want to see a deep level of involvement and a true contribution to the school and community around you.

Your Demonstrated Interest: Medium Importance

Thanks to the Common App, it's easier than ever to apply to multiple colleges. That's why schools are taking a closer look at your real interest in them. Ways to demonstrate interest include visiting the campus and introducing yourself to faculty and staff, meeting with admission representatives who visit your school, maintaining contact with the admissions office via social media, registering with the college at a College Fair, and applying Early Decision or Early Action. Make sure to sign in so the college knows you were there; they keep records.

Counselor and Teacher Recommendation: Medium Importance

A generic recommendation doesn't carry much weight for admissions officers who are looking for personalized insight on a student. Unfortunately, too, admissions offices are seeing more and more of these. In fact, now some schools offer boxes for high school guidance counselors to check off that they don't know enough about a student to give a recommendation or that they don't have enough time to fill out the form. Reasons given are that they are overwhelmed with requests or they have too many students to get to know them all. I strongly recommend that you get to know your guidance counselor and one or two teachers well. Recommendations still count, and if it comes down to you and a similar student, a recommendation or two with thoughtful comments can put you ahead.

Interviews: Medium Importance

Many selective colleges offer interviews. An interview can help you make a good impression, but it is rarely a deciding factor in whether you get admitted. Interviews usually confirm an overall impression. Alternatively, a terrible interview can hurt your acceptance chances, especially if you're in the maybe pile.

Senior Year: Super-High Importance for Students Applying for January Deadlines and Students on a Wait-List

Colleges no longer tolerate slacking off during the senior year. In fact, some want to see "acceleration of educational difficulty." You've spent eleven years getting to where you are; don't blow it in the twelfth!

Application Auditing: High Importance

I'm putting this near the end because it's about the things you shouldn't do rather than what you should do. Don't plagiarize. Chances are that you will get caught, thanks to technology. A growing number of colleges are fact-checking applications. Colleges also might look at your Facebook profile and other online presence to see if your activities match your claims.

Responding on Time: High Importance

If a college sends you an email, respond with whatever information is being requested. And use professional writing. No " GR8s" or other informal spellings.

ADDITIONAL FACTORS

Underrepresented Applicants

Schools crave diversity. This gives them advantages in the rankings and makes for a more educational atmosphere, as in you'll have different peers to learn from. Gender, race, ethnicity, religion, age, geographic origin, talents, and more can make you different than the rest. For example, a desired minority group is women who are interested in engineering or the sciences. I had two top admissions officers say to me, "If you have a female interested in science, we want them to consider our school!"

In-State/Out-of-State Status

If you are applying to most public institutions, state residency will usually give you an admission edge over out-of-state applicants. However, with budget cuts, this is changing: Many public colleges are wooing and appreciating the out-of-state and even out-of-country tuition. All state schools will publish their in- state vs. out-of-state acceptance rate and profile for applications.

Legacy Status

Children of graduates often get a preferred status in the selection process. Sometimes grandchildren, nieces and nephews, and cousins do, too. This varies from school to school, and if you're counting on this to give you the edge you need, it's worth calling the admissions office and asking them to define legacy status. Keep in mind, relations won't make up for poor grades or test scores—UNLESS perhaps your family's last name is on a campus building.

Special Talents

Students with exceptional talents may receive special admission consideration. A special talent may be in music, sports, writing, photography, etc. If you have a special talent, write about it in your application. Along with having the talent, you must meet basic academic standards.

Recruited Athletes

In the last thirty years, college athletics has changed into a multi-billion dollar business. Recruiting student athletes has become strategic and competitive, especially in sports like football and basketball where a championship could potentially increase undergraduate admissions and booster donations. Coaches will "go to bat" for certain student athletes in a wide range of sports.

CHOOSING THE RIGHT HIGH SCHOOL CLASSES

Regardless of who you are, you must choose your high school classes carefully. While there's no 100-percent-guaranteed future college admissions formula, there are a few strong patterns for success.

Meet the high school requirements.

High schools have a list of required credits that must be taken in order to graduate. Colleges don't look favorably on students who weren't organized enough to graduate.

Take a balanced set of classes.

Typically, a student should try to take courses each year in English, science, math, the social sciences, and foreign language.

Choose a smart range of college-prep courses.

A student doesn't need to take Advanced Placement (AP) Everything to get into college, but course choice depends on the selectivity of the colleges a student wants to attend. Demanding and challenging honors, accelerated, AP, and International Baccalaureate (IB) courses make a student more desirable to a school. However, colleges recognize a student can only take advantage of accelerated courses if their high school provides them. If AP courses or International Baccalaureate programs are not offered at a high school, colleges understand and only expect that a student will excel in the opportunities to which there is access. Colleges also understand different schools have different requirements that may restrict what courses a student can take.

Show colleges a positive pattern.

Colleges like to see a high level (or an improving degree) of rigor and success throughout a student's high school years. This includes the senior year. Have you heard this famous question: "Is it better to take a course where I know I can get an 'A,' or should I take a harder course and risk getting a lower grade?" The answer is: "It's best to get an 'A' in a harder course." Students need to seek challenge, not avoid it, and succeed in the challenges chosen.

Know the admissions guidelines for top-choice colleges.

Many colleges, especially the selective ones, have specific admissions requirements for entering students—for example, a foreign language requirement. It is best to research each school individually. Make sure you meet any and all minimum requirements.

Pursue intellectual interests.

It's OK to take courses of a personal interest like filmmaking or fashion; just make sure it is not at the expense of a schedule's overall rigor. Honesty is very important when deciding between different courses. Are you choosing drama because you have a real excitement about it and the challenge it presents, or is the motivation powered by a desire to avoid a different (and perhaps difficult) academic subject?

Consult with teachers, a high school counselor, and/or a college advisor on what courses are most appropriate.

Some difficult decisions may also need to be made about which courses to take and how to balance schoolwork and extracurricular activities.

Chapter 2:

Overview of the Application Process

Take a deep breath.

The college application is hard.

But, it's hard for a reason. The colleges are testing you. They want to know if you have what it takes to go to them.

The trick it not to look at the process as one giant, over-whelming whole, but a series of bite-sized pieces.

GETTING STARTED

Keep pertinent information easily accessible.
Print out the following and put it in an expandable folder. Then don't lose track of the folder.

- Your social security number.

- Financial aid plans. (Do you intend to apply for need-based financial aid or merit-based scholarships?)

- Family information— your parents' or guardians' legal names, addresses, occupations, employers, colleges they attended, years they graduated, and degrees they hold.

- Your high school's information—address, your date of entry to the school, and your guidance counselor's full name and contact information.

- Scores on standardized tests (SAT/ACT) or AP test scores.

- A list of the high school courses you're currently enrolled in.

- A credit card for the payment of the application and to send the test scores.

Track all dates and deadlines on a calendar.
You can do this on an old-fashioned wall/desk calendar or program the dates into your phone and set it up to alert you as the deadlines approach.

Keep a folder for each college of interest to you.
This will help ensure that you keep all the printed materials, notes, correspondence, passwords, and photos together. They will all start running together otherwise. Whenever you send an email to a school or interviewer, or receive a response, make sure you print it out and add it to the folder. You will also want to take screenshots of completed applications and confirmations. One of our students used a screenshot to prove his application was not late. And it worked. It's best to keep all this together.

Break down your tasks. Set manageable goals for yourself.
You won't be able to complete the application in one night or even one weekend. And if you take it all on at one time, it's going to be overwhelming. Pick a date for contacting teachers, counselors, or coaches who are writing recommendations. Set your own deadlines for one or two scholarships at a time. Set a time with your parents to complete the financial aid form, FAFSA. (There's a detailed description of the FAFSA in Chapter 18.)

INTERNATIONAL COLLEGE COUNSELORS TIP: Send all applications in at least one month prior to the Priority Deadlines. This way, you can confirm receipt and resend any missing documents.

Plan ahead when it comes to transcripts and recommendations. Some high schools send colleges your transcripts over the computer. Other schools make students fill out a paper form and will send the transcripts by mail. For safety and sanity, visit your guidance counselor's office, find out your school's way of doing things, and make the request at least two months before a deadline.

Send your test scores in on time.

Students must request that test scores be sent to all of their colleges by the deadline. At most schools, your application will not be considered without your scores.

Here's where to sign up for standardized tests and request your scores:
SAT score information:　　　　http://sat.collegeboard.org/scores
ACT score information:
　　http://www.actstudent.org/scores/send/asrphone.html

Surround yourself with the right people.
These happen to be other students who are eagerly researching colleges and really working hard on their applications. Seeing and hearing others who are submitting applications and excited about opportunities will motivate you to complete your own. You may also learn about schools and scholarship opportunities from them.

AN APPLICATION OVERVIEW

The Common Application
With the Common Application, you can fill out one application and submit it to all participating schools.

The Common Application has over 500 members in forty-eight states and the District of Columbia, as well as in Austria, France, Germany, Italy, the United Kingdom, and Switzerland. This number makes it the dominant electronic site for submitting applications to colleges.
　　https://www.commonapp.org

The Universal College Application
The Universal College Application has thirty-three member colleges. Like the Common Application, one application can be sent to many schools.
　　https://www.universalcollegeapp.com

Common Black College Application

The EDU, Inc. Application allows you to complete one application and have it submitted to over 30 historically black colleges and universities (HBCUs) at the same time for only $35.

http:/www.eduinconline.com/index.html

State- and School-Specific Electronic Applications

A number of colleges and universities have their own applications that can be found on their website.

INTERNATIONAL COLLEGE COUNSELORS TIP: Fill out the appropriate application for the school. Both the Common Application and Universal College Application websites have lists of member colleges and universities.

COLLEGE APPLICATION HINTS AND TIPS

Triple-check even the basic information.

This means your name, address, Social Security number, birth date, and email. Make sure that your name is spelled correctly and consistently on your applications and official documents. Misspellings and nicknames can lead colleges to think that two different people exist. Ask someone else to look it over before you send it out, just in case you missed something.

Print-preview your application.

Do this before you hit send. Do a PDF view to make sure that your complete answer shows up. If you don't see it, neither will the admissions officers.

Write all the essays, and write them right.

Make sure you send in all the essays requested by a school and keep the essay lengths to the guidelines specified.

Submit all parts of the application.

If you are applying through the Common Application and do not submit the supplement, your application is incomplete. If you forget to send official test scores, transcripts from all schools you have attended, and recommendation letters as required by individual schools, your application is also incomplete. Make sure everything is submitted before the deadline.

Track deadlines and submit early.

There is absolutely no reason for your application to be late. The deadlines are clearly posted on admissions office websites. Convince yourself that your application is due at least a month before the deadline. Servers crash and weather happens. There is no "Act of G-d" clause that will drive a college to accept your application after the deadline.

Follow up.

Once you submit your application, most schools will send you a school ID and login information to check on your application status. Do this immediately and keep track of what pieces are missing. When you send missing pieces in, follow up on them too. For schools without an online confirmation system, send a simple email a week or two after you submit your complete application saying, "I want to confirm you received my application and all supporting documents." Be sure to include your application with such a correspondence.

Don't assume your counselor will take care of something.

Many colleges do not send counselors alerts, so an independent counselor or high school counselor will not know if any information is missing from your application. You and you alone have the final responsibility for making sure the college or scholarship has everything it needs. (See "Follow up" above.) It's all part of the "Are you worthy?" test.

Follow directions.

If a school or scholarship says it needs something by a certain deadline, send it in by the deadline. If it says an essay should be 500 words or less, make it close to 500 words or less. What the college wants, the college should get. Don't second-guess the admissions office. If you are submitting your application online, the box you type your essay into may cut you off after the maximum number of words. Make sure you do not paste in your essay and send it in without double-checking to see what has been saved.

VIP APPLICATIONS: WHAT ARE THEY?

Every fall, a number of high school seniors will receive a personalized e-mail or letter congratulating them for qualifying for a special "VIP Application."

These applications are sent from colleges to select students encouraging them to attend the school. The VIP Applications offer a fast-track, simplified application process and often stress the offer being good for a "limited time."

Select students are typically those with high SAT scores and academic high-achievers. Some schools send these applications to students who merely registered to take the SAT, live in a certain zip code, requested information, or visited campus.

VIP Applications also come under the names "Presidential Select," "Select Scholar," "Priority Application," and others.

Ultimately, these special applications are a marketing ploy with benefits for both the school and the student. These applications help increase a school's applicant pool. For students, VIP Applications are quick and easy to fill out. Many times the student's name and address are already filled in. Typically they don't require a long essay and applying is free.

An acceptance is not a binding commitment. It's also worth noting that receiving a VIP Application is not a guarantee that you will be accepted.

If you received a VIP Application, feel flattered and complete it if you have some interest in the school. It's a good opportunity of which to take advantage. Students often get the chance to receive an early acceptance to a school, and having an early acceptance can ease anxiety. Though, if you're not a good fit for the school, you should spend your time elsewhere. You'll have plenty to do without chasing the red herrings.

HOW TO AVOID APPLICATION FEES AND SAVE MONEY!

College applications can cost between $35 and $80 each. But there are ways to avoid the fees:

Apply to a school with no application fee.
Mississippi's Millsaps College is one without a fee. Others are Johnson & Wales University, Lewis & Clark College, Smith College, and Eastern Nazarene College.

Demonstrate financial need.
Most schools will waive the application fee for students with financial need. To be eligible for a fee waiver, some qualifications include: you have received or are eligible to receive an ACT or SAT testing fee waiver; you are enrolled or eligible to enroll in the Federal Free or Reduced Price Lunch program; your family receives public assistance; your family income falls within the Income Eligibility Guidelines set by the USDA and Nutrition Service; or you are a ward of the state or an orphan. Oftentimes students will need a signed statement from their school official, college access counselor, financial aid officer, or community leader confirming that they and their family cannot afford to pay the application fee. Read each school's application fee information carefully.

Be a legacy, sibling, or family member of an alumnus.
At some schools, like Barry University, University of Richmond, and Butler University, being a relative of an alum can get you a free application. Call and ask the school.

Visit the school.
Some schools offer an application waiver as "appreciation" for making the effort to visit. Alfred University is one. Penn State (other than the University Park campus) is another one. Make sure you schedule an appointment. Also find out the school's policy on application waivers

in advance. Some schools require you to submit it while you're on campus.

Call the school and ask.

Some schools offer application waivers during certain time periods of the year. Others will give you a fee waiver with an alumni recommendation. Then there are other schools that will give you a waiver if you ask nicely.

DEADLINES

Early Policies. They can maximize your chances to get into a school, but you need to read them carefully.

The names sound similar, but there are huge differences. You do not want to get caught violating school policies, so be sure to read and understand the rules for each school.

Early Decision
Binding
Students can apply Early Decision to only one college. "Binding" means that you agree to attend the college if it accepts you and offers adequate financial aid. If you're accepted via Early Decision, you must withdraw all other applications. Students who aren't accepted early, and are not rejected, are still considered with the regular applicant pool. The typical Early Decision deadline is late October to late November. If you want to compare financial aid packages, do not apply Early Decision.

Early Decision II
Binding
This is similar to Early Decision, but with a later deadline. The acceptance rate for Early Decision is generally higher than it is for regular decisions regardless of whether the deadline is earlier or later. The typical deadline is January 1 or January 15.

23

Early Action
Nonbinding

Early Action is not binding, meaning students who get accepted do not have to commit. The typical deadline is late October to late November. Usually, Early Action has few restrictions and benefits the student by allowing them to hear early from a school.

Single-Choice Early Action/Restrictive Early Action
Nonbinding

You can apply early to only one school—but the decision is nonbinding. See each school's website, as there are some differences among the restrictions. For example, in some cases you can still apply to public colleges or to college scholarship programs.

Priority Admissions/Priority Deadline
Nonbinding

Priority admissions is just like the regular deadline. After that deadline has passed, schools accept applications on a case-by-case scenario.

Regular Decision
Nonbinding

Your application gets sent in for the regular admission pool. Most students apply for regular decision. The typical deadline is December 15–January 15. Students who get accepted do not have to commit.

Rolling Admissions
Nonbinding

The school reviews applications as they are completed. A number of schools, particularly big state schools, use rolling admissions. Check each school's rolling admissions start date. Some schools accept applications as early as the summer before the senior year. Under rolling admissions, colleges accept eligible candidates until all freshman spots are filled—so the earlier you apply, the better. Students typically receive the decision within two months after the completed application is sent in. Students who get accepted do not have to commit, and some schools give students until May 1 to make a decision.

Guaranteed Admissions

Offered by a number of public universities to students who meet certain academic and/or test score requirements. Students still need to apply, but qualified candidates typically get admissions offers earlier than other students.

Early Notification/Early Evaluation

An option offered to applicants by a limited number of selective institutions and is designed to give students an idea of their chances for admission. This is not an admission plan, nor is it an offer of admission.

WHEN TO APPLY TO COLLEGE UTILIZING EARLY DECISION/ EARLY ACTION

Only students who are absolutely certain they know which school they want to attend should apply Early Decision.

Early Action is a good option for students who would like to know if they got into a school sooner rather than later. Students accepted under Early Action can typically wait until May 1 to decide where to enroll.

Benefits of applying early may include:

▸ Improving your chance of being accepted

▸ Improving your chance of getting a scholarship

▸ Getting first choice for housing

▸ Gaining time to prepare for college and study for high school classes/AP tests, if accepted

▸ Gaining more time to apply to other colleges with later deadlines if you get rejected

▸ Receiving peace of mind

Early Decision and Financial Aid

If you are admitted early, but unhappy with the financial aid awarded, you can make an appeal. Be careful of the pitfall in doing this: your high school is not permitted to send your transcripts to other colleges when an early decision offer is still in play. You may have to wait awhile for the school to process your appeal.

You do have the option of backing out of the binding agreement if you aren't offered a sufficient financial aid package. You can even reapply under regular decision and hope for a better financial aid package.

Chapter 3:
Social Media, You, and College Admissions

I decided to add this chapter into the book sooner rather than later so you'd be able to get a head start on cleaning up your online presence.

College admissions officers use Facebook and Twitter! They read blogs, check out YouTube, and view Instagram photos and videos.

The horror stories are true of students being denied admission or scholarships thanks to something they posted online. Sports team coaches also like to check out potential athletes. Colleges and coaches want responsible students, not ones who may bring trouble. Don't be fooled into thinking "private" pages are private. The way security keeps changing, your best bet is not to post anything you think can embarrass you.

Common sense is key.

Here are some general guidelines for keeping admissions chances safe:

Do not write anything negative about colleges.
One student praised the school while visiting the campus then trashed it online. Admissions took notice, and the student was rejected.

Never post anything online that is incriminating or embarrassing. Ever.
Representatives have reported receiving anonymous Facebook and Google "tips" around admissions time, including photos of students doing things that they shouldn't be doing. On at least one occasion, a tip has caused an offer of admission to be revoked. (Some tips are called in by jealous classmates [frenemies] also vying for an Ivy League school.)

Check your "tags."
Check to see if any Facebook "friends" who have access to their profile have posted any unflattering comments or tagged questionable photos

with their name. If there is something they do not want to be connected to, students must untag themselves and talk to the person who posted the pictures and ask to have them taken down.

Remove phone numbers and addresses from Facebook.
This makes it harder to do a search on you. It's a safety guideline as well.

Set privacy filters as strongly as possible.
But never assume that what you post will not be seen. (See #2.)

Use the "grandparent test."
If you wouldn't want your grandparents to see what was posted online, then it should not be posted. This goes for things on a personal wall or webpage, or someone else's. Make sure your friends know about this test policy, too. (If your grandparents happen to be wild and crazy folks, err on the side of conservative caution.)

Remove all photos and posts with anything questionable, including:

- Drinking and/or drugs, even if you're abstaining—this includes holding a cup of any kind

- Wild behavior, even if alcohol or drugs aren't in the picture

- Nudity

- Hints of sex or sexuality

- The X-rated and the R-rated

- Interests that are questionable

- Favorite quotes that reference illegal activities

- Obscene or offensive language, gestures and activities

- Bullying, cheating, or lying

- Anything else you might regret

Let your friends know not to post anything that might get you into trouble either.

The Positive Side of Social Media

With the negatives come positives, too. There's an opportunity to present yourself positively. Online, you can distinguish yourself by showcasing your achievements and accomplishments, and/or revealing some of your goals and aspirations. Athletes can post highlight videos. Film students can post their work. Science students can present a project they are working on.

At International College Counselors, we encourage students to use online presence and social networking tools to their advantage. Many colleges do look at student pages and blogs, especially if those students are being considered for a scholarship. The more prestigious the scholarship, the more they'll scrutinize.

Furthermore, students can use social media to express interest in the colleges to which they are applying. "Friend" a college's Facebook page, become a Twitter follower, or join a college's LinkedIn group. Students can even contact an admissions representative directly. If you do this, be polite and respectful of the rep's time. Some schools also offer social media outreach that lets prospective students interact with current students.

PROFESSIONALIZE YOUR EMAIL ADDRESS

If your email address begins with "partygirl" or "wilddude," it's time to open another email address, even if you only use it for college applications and jobs. Then, if you have to make up something, make up something nice like "taylorincollege." A name like "gatorhater" should not be used to apply to the University of Florida—or any other school either. A memorable email address or your first and last name is better than a long string of numbers and letters. Make sure you check your inbox regularly so you don't miss anything from the colleges to which you've applied.

Chapter 4:
Writing Essays

TIPS FOR WRITING THE COLLEGE ESSAY

The personal essay can help you improve your chances for admission.

Your essay may be as short as 150 words, but the words you choose can mean the difference between a "maybe" and a "yes." Your writing tells the admissions committee how and why you are different from everybody else.

While there is no exact formula for the perfect admission essay, here are some tips you should consider when trying to make a lasting impression on someone who reads 50 to 100 essays a day:

Write about yourself.
The admissions committee isn't looking to learn about the American Revolution or bioresearch, they're looking to learn about you—your achievements, your obstacles, your goals, your passions, your personality, your values, and your character. If you are asked to write about an influential person, the college wants to know his or her influence on you. Whatever topic you choose to center your essay around, make sure you shine through.

Focus on one facet of yourself.
Admissions committees are looking for an in-depth essay. Pick one project, one activity, or one passion. Don't try to cover too many topics in your essay, or you'll end up with a laundry list of details and activities. The magic is in the details. Make the reader remember you.

Tell a good story.
Demonstrate how you are compassionate—don't just tell readers you are. If you had a difficulty, don't give the admissions committee a laundry list of complaints. Tell them how you overcame them.

Keep it real.

Don't make things up or try to come across as someone completely different than yourself. If you speak from the heart, it will show and your essay will flow more easily. Choosing something you've experienced will also give you the vivid and specific details the admissions committee is looking to see in your essay.

Share your opinions, but avoid anything controversial.

You don't know who is going to be reading your essay, so you want to appeal to the broadest audience possible. Write about something you like as opposed to something you don't. This is not the time or the place to share your opinions on what's wrong with a government or argue about religion. Don't disparage (SAT word alert) any people, concepts, or ideas.

Don't repeat information already in your application.

If you've taken six AP courses in one year, don't list that you've done it or that you did it because you "love to learn" unless this relates directly to the focus of your essay. Admissions officers want to learn something about you from your essay that they can't learn from reading the other sections of your application.

Leverage your native culture, traditions, and experiences.

If you're an international applicant, Native American, or otherwise non-traditional student, don't try to "Americanize" or "mainstream" your application. Schools are looking for diversity. The goal is to stand out and not appear to be like all the other applicants.

Add a little something about the school.

Mention something specific about the school, especially something academic. For example, note whether you're interested in a certain major, program, track, or professor. Don't over-flatter the school or talk about generic features like a beautiful campus or dining hall. Adding something about the school's academic programs shows you did research and there's a scholarly reason you're applying there.

Copy-and-paste carefully.

It's easier to tailor one essay for many schools than to write each one from scratch. Besides, most schools will ask similar questions: for example, why you want to attend or study a particular major. So you're cutting and pasting. However, read every essay over carefully, like it's the first one you wrote. Almost every admission officer can tell tales of students who accidentally wrote how excited they were by the opportunities offered at another school. Admissions officers understand that you are applying to more than their college. However, this kind of mistake demonstrates carelessness, and they don't like that. Not one bit. Especially if you told the other college it was your first choice.

Avoid scientific words, acronyms, industry jargon, or foreign phrases.

Avoid using them if you can. Your essay needs to be easy for anyone to read. If the name of a club or school magazine is not instantly recognizable for what it is, add a short description. You write for *Embryo*. What is that? Write down *Embryo*, the school literary magazine. As smart as admissions readers are, you also cannot assume that they know all the latest words or complex industry terms.

OMG!

Avoid using slang or other hard-to-decipher language. The clearer you are with what you want to convey, the better.

Profanity

Don't use any. It will get you noticed. Not in a good way.

Spend time on your essay.

Hemingway didn't write his stories overnight, and neither should you write your essay overnight. The admission committee is looking to see what you can do given the time to brainstorm, rewrite, and polish. They are looking to see what topic you chose and what you did with it. An essay won't help you if it's sloppy and uninformative.

Check your grammar and spelling.

Yes, this counts. You can write conversationally, but the grammar and spelling still need to be correct. And don't solely rely on your computer's spell-checker. Often times, the wrong word (spelled correctly) can slip by. Nothing says last-minute essay more than the wrong spelling and grammar.

Show the essay to someone who can give you objective feedback.

Sometimes you can get too close to the essay and be unable to see it clearly. Other people can often tell if there isn't enough being revealed, or your essay rambles, or if the humor is falling flat, or if you're not making the impression you'd want to. Remember, this essay is going to someone who doesn't know you and is going to be making a big decision based on what they'll learn from it.

COMMON APPLICATION ESSAYS

The Common Application is a single college application that students can complete and send to any number of participating colleges. For the 2013–14 application cycle, the Common Application asked students to choose one of the following essay prompts and write an essay that is between 250 to 650 words:

▸ Some students have a background or story that is so central to their identity that they believe their application would be incomplete without it. If this sounds like you, then please share your story.

▸ Recount an incident or time when you experienced failure. How did it affect you, and what lessons did you learn?

▸ Reflect on a time when you challenged a belief or idea. What prompted you to act? Would you make the same decision again?

▸ Describe a place or environment where you are perfectly content. What do you do or experience there, and why is it meaningful to you?

▸ Discuss an accomplishment or event, formal or informal, that marked your transition from childhood to adulthood within your culture, community, or family.

In all of these essay prompts, students should find the key words and emphasize on these. Some key words that should start your thoughts include "background," "story," "incident," "failure," "lessons learned," "challenged," "place or environment," "experience," "accomplishment," "culture, community, or family," etc.

How to Start an Essay

Start with an idea of what you want to say. Remember your audience—a college that values academics, civic engagement, and cultural sensitivity. Maybe you want to talk about your volunteer work or growing up as a member of a minority group. Write, write, and keep writing. Don't worry about word count. Don't worry if you stray from your original thought. Don't worry about over- sharing or going too much into detail. When your brain runs dry, read over what you wrote. Pick out the things you think sound interesting. Then see how you can work it to meet the essay's guidelines.

THE OPTIONAL ESSAY

Optional essays aren't optional. Some students believe that they can opt to ignore the optional essay. It's one of those trick "questions." Don't opt out.

If you are unsure about what to include, talk to your parents, a college counselor, a teacher, or a mentor.

Typically, I recommend that students explain their personal circumstances in the optional essay/additional information and use the main essay to highlight other, more positive, experiences—unless the challenge was life-changing. I also recommend leaving some details out. For example, if you faced a challenge that did not reflect significantly on your schoolwork or extracurricular activities, you may want to leave this out. One essay that comes to mind was one I saw on an eating disorder. The struggle was a major part of her life, but it was going to distract an admissions officer from her other accomplishments.

INTERNATIONAL COLLEGE COUNSELORS TIP: Always think about what information you want colleges to know and use when evaluating your application. This should guide you in what to share. Don't share anything that doesn't put you in the best light, unless you absolutely have to, or you can turn it around to show the positive.

Writing about setbacks: What do you say? How do you say it?

If your grades or involvement in activities dropped significantly at some point in your high school career, somewhere in your application you need to explain why. You can explain this in the main essay or in the section "additional information." Many colleges leave space for the descriptions of unusual circumstances.

Whatever you do, do not turn your essay into something designed to score pity points. Many other students have had to deal with real hardships too.

The essay you write should demonstrate to colleges that despite the challenges you faced, you were able to stay focused and to overcome them. Admissions officers want an explanation of the situation, but as important is how you dealt with it.

If you talk about a challenge, it has to truly have affected you while in high school. Moving cross-country or having to work two jobs to support your family while attending school is something to share. Getting sick and missing a few tests is not. Trying to make something major out of something minor can demonstrate questionable judgment. If you provide no explanation to sudden grade drops, the admissions officers will draw their own conclusions. Expect that this will not work in your favor.

Own up to any bad behavior.

Don't lie about school punishments. Your high school is duty-bound to report them. And don't pretend your suspension for boozing it up at a football game was a one-time thing if you had two warnings beforehand. This will also be reported. What matters to the college is how you processed your experience. Colleges want to see that you accept responsibility for your actions, show sincere remorse, and/or can talk about what lessons you've learned. From our experience, a student who admits wrongdoing in an honest and apologetic way can be extremely successful with college admissions.

ANSWERING THE QUIRKY QUESTIONS

In recent years, a number of colleges have been adding quirky questions to their applications. These supplemental questions are considered a way to get students to stand out from the crowd.

These questions have included:

- Imagine you have to wear a costume for a year of your life. What would you pick and why?

- What is your favorite ride at the amusement park? How does this reflect your approach to life?

- What does Play-Doh have to do with Plato?

- What would you do with a free afternoon tomorrow?

- What was your favorite thing about last Tuesday?

- The Spanish poet Antonio Machado wrote, "Between living and dreaming there is a third thing. Guess it." Give us your guess.

- According to Henry David Thoreau, "One is not born into the world to do everything, but to do something." What is your something?

What colleges are looking for is your voice. Use this as an opportunity to demonstrate your "out-of-the-box" thinking. However, don't go overboard. Admissions officers are looking to see if you'll be an interesting person to have on campus. Interesting means imaginative, not crazy and not dangerous sounding.

GREAT FIRST SENTENCES

You need a great hook and a great first sentence. Opening sentences have the power to compel and fascinate. Some of our favorite student first sentences include:

- *For eight years, I have celebrated polyester.*

- *I vividly recall coming home from school one day in Buenos Aires, Argentina, to find my house in disarray and my parents packing one suitcase after another.*

- *I'll admit it: I have a thing for gavels—a thing for motions and seconds and the clarity that they bring to meetings.*

- *I eagerly reached into my Hello Kitty backpack.*

- *Max prances in place as we await our turn into the arena.*

- *Drip. Drip. Drip. Tick. Tick. Tick. As I lie in the hospital, waiting to be taken into surgery, I can only think that my IV drip sounds just like a metronome.*

You want to read more, right?

FATAL ESSAY ERRORS

Application essays have been requested as part of the college application for the past umpteen years. The admissions teams have seen a lot of "creativity." Here are their least favorite types of essays:

- Metaphor. Don't compare yourself to a mango, a Ferris wheel, or any other objects.

- Death. Don't write about a person or pet's death unless it truly affected your life and you can use it to exemplify growth—for example, if someone died of cancer and you made it your mission to raise money/awareness, or if a death during high school affected your grades and caused you to stumble, but then you regrouped to overcome.

- Free verse essays, essays written as raps, limericks, etc. Don't emphasize form over function.

- "Meta" essays where you talk about writing an essay, about the process of writing an essay, or about essays themselves.

Additionally, you should avoid writing about the topics below unless you have something extraordinary to say:

- A trip to Europe
- Generic admiration for your mom or dad
- The controversial rock star or movie star who you idolize
- Overcoming an injury and making an athletic comeback
- Volunteering at a local community center
- Building homes in Costa Rica with Habit for Humanity
- Understanding the meaning of life from a fishing trip

Sorry, but thousands of students have beat you to these topics and then beaten them to death. These are called "cliché essays" because the reader knows from the get-go just where you are going with it.

THE VIDEO COLLEGE ESSAY

A number of college admissions departments are formally accepting video college essays.

The first step for any student is to view recent videos and see what others have done. This will give you an idea of the range of possibilities.

When it comes to actually making your video, it's important to be original but in a way that is comfortable for you. Do what works for you. Your main goal needs to be communicating your message.

- Start by identifying the question and any directions.
- Think about what you want to say.

- Write a script that is clear on the message and ideas you want to get across.

- Collect resources and props that you want to use in the video.

- Record the video until it's as perfect as possible. Some students record the video themselves using a tripod and speaking directly into the camera, others enlist the services of a friend or family member.

- Review your video and collect feedback.

- Edit, edit, edit, and re-record if necessary.

- Get more feedback.

- Edit and re-record until it's as perfect as it can be. Make sure it fits the requested length and meets all specs before sending it in.

TRUTH, PLAGIARISM, AND THE CONSEQUENCES ON COLLEGE APPLICATIONS AND ESSAYS

No matter how desperately you want to get into a school, don't lie on the college application. If a university finds out you lied on an application or essay—even a little—you will get rejected, almost guaranteed.

How does a school know if a student fibbed/fudged/lied? Colleges are doing research of their own. A common practice is for college admissions officers to call up high schools to verify a student's activities and awards. College admissions officers have also called employers, internship organizers, and places where students have performed public service. They are also looking applicants up online.

Thanks to the Internet, it's easy to see if a student really has received a major award or a significant ranking, whether it's in music or sports. Some universities like MIT have even hired private investigators to check up on student claims. While there is always a chance you won't be caught, do you really want to risk it?

39

Embellishing the truth isn't particularly good either. If you delivered meals to homebound senior citizens in their community, don't write that you ended world hunger. Of course, there's nothing wrong with presenting yourself in a positive way. This is where ethics (and clever adjectives) need to kick in.

Plagiarism is always wrong, and schools are getting better at detecting it. Stanford and Penn State, for example, are using an admissions essay service offered by Turnitin. This software service is used by a number of professors to check their students' class work, and it has proven to be a big success. College application essays are now being compared to a huge database of collected information and what's already on the web. While most schools don't publicize whether or not they use this detection system, students have been rejected because of plagiarism on the college application.

College essays are about the student: who they are and not who they're not. I truly believe that every student has a gem of an essay within them. What they need to do is find that ounce of truth and turn it into a ton of good, positive writing. Remember to proofread.

Chapter 5:
Letters of Recommendation

One of the most important parts of your college application isn't even written by you, and that's the Letters of Recommendation section.

Do not wait until the last minute to get these. You should actually be working on getting letters of recommendation from the minute you start a school year.

You want the college admissions officers to know that a teacher or other recommender is really recommending you for a school, not just going through the motions.

WHO SHOULD YOU ASK FOR A LETTER OF RECOMMEND-ATION?

When it comes to choosing whom to ask, you want adults—unrelated to you—who know you well enough to write something special about you. Most private colleges want one counselor and two teacher recommendations.

The best recommendations provide insight about you and knowledge of your high school success, so you want to ask people who can write about your talents, abilities, and more. For example, teachers can comment about your academic skills, but it's better if they can comment on your personality too.

Believe it or not, admissions officers have seen the same letter for different students—with the names changed, of course. What happened is that more than one student from a school applied to the same college and asked the same teacher for a recommendation. Apparently, the teacher didn't know either student too well and wrote something generic and uninspired.

So choose a teacher who knows you over a teacher who gave you top grades, or one who you think can "write well." For example, your

English teacher may write the best, but a strong letter of recommendation supporting you goes a lot further than a letter that has perfect grammar, but no substance.

Choose the person you ask wisely and carefully. Make sure you choose someone who likes you. If you ask a teacher, make sure it's in a class where you have great attendance, few or no tardies, actively participate in class, are well behaved, and get good grades. You may not even see the letter that is written about you, so it needs to be from someone you feel comfortable with.

On the Common Application, you are not able to make changes to the teacher/counselor list after you submit your application, with the exception of resending the notification to your teacher or counselor. So make sure before you push the submit button that you have wisely selected your recommenders.

INTERNATIONAL COLLEGE COUNSELORS TIP: Almost all schools ask for a counselor recommendation. Be sure to get to know your counselor and provide her with the information she needs to know about you.

TREND ALERT: PARENT RECOMMENDATIONS

A small number of colleges are welcoming letters of recommendation from parents. The colleges that do this are looking for parents to bring a new dimension to candidates whose full personality may otherwise be captured only with grades, test scores, and traditional recommendation letters from teachers and guidance counselors. Only a few colleges want these; if a college does not ask for this, do not send a parent-written recommendation in.

HOW TO ASK FOR A LETTER OF RECOMMENDATION

Carefully read the instructions on what kind of letters of recommendation each school requires. Some applications require two letters of recommendation from teachers and one counselor recommendation. Other applications ask for one teacher recommendation and one counselor recommendation, or that you choose teachers from specific subjects like English and Math. Other applications allow you to choose an employer or a friend. Make sure you follow the directions!

Start early.

Two months before an application deadline, start asking for your letters of recommendation. Your recommender needs time to write a thoughtful and articulate letter. Consider asking teachers prior to the summer. This will give them plenty of time to write something reflective and complete.

Make an appointment to speak with your recommenders.

Don't just thrust the letter template into a teacher's hand in the five minutes you have between periods or tackle a coach in the locker room. Making an appointment shows that you're respectful of their time.

Help your recommender.

At your meeting, make sure you give those chosen people everything they might need to write your letter and submit it on time. You gain extra points for yourself because your letter will, more likely, be properly detailed. You gain extra points with recommenders for showing them that you are taking this process seriously and that you appreciate their time and effort.

Be careful about sending a teacher your resume. You want him or her to write about you as a student in a particular class. You don't want them listing your activities.

Follow up.

Remember, your recommenders are doing you a favor. Show your appreciation by sending a thank-you note.

Chapter 6:
Interviewing and Resumes

There are two types of college interviews.

One is a formal or traditional interview. This interview takes place on or off campus with a dean or an admissions officer. Generally, the interviewer will ask you questions and you will answer them. The school wants to get a sense of you, find out how much thinking you have done about college, and learn how well you express yourself and perform in an interview situation.

The second is the informal or alumni interview. This interview is more conversational. In an informal interview, the interviewer wants to get a sense of your interests and how well you would fit in on campus.

It's important to know which type of interview(s) a school has.

Practice and knowing what to expect will help you through both kinds of interviews.

Many colleges no longer require interviews, but interviews can give a student the edge if the school is forced to choose between closely matched applicants.

ARE INTERVIEWS REQUIRED?

Each school has different requirements. Not every college you apply to will require an interview. However, do not assume a school does not require an interview.

Read your application materials closely to see if an interview is required or recommended.

No two schools are exactly alike. At many schools, interviews don't count towards admissions. Their interviews are "informative."

Other schools have an evaluative interview, which means they "count." Double-check a college's requirements by calling the admissions office. If an interview is not required but recommended, give it a go.

However, we don't always recommend the interview for our students. If you are exceptionally shy, insecure, or really truly believe your nervousness or lack of social skills will make a poor impression, do not go on an interview unless it is mandatory. It is better to let your application do the talking for you. While an interview can help, it can also hurt an application.

SETTING UP AN INTERVIEW

Some colleges want the students to call them or fill out an online form to set up the interview. So the first thing you need to do is call the admissions office or check online to find out what the school interview policy is.

The interview should take place before the application deadline, November or December for most schools. The interview appointment should be set about one month before you plan to do the interview. Two, three, or even four months in advance works too. It's better to err on the early side. The worst that can happen is that the school will tell you it's too early to make an appointment and they'll tell you when to call back. Some schools, like Yale, have a limited number of on- campus interviews that are available on a first-come, first-served basis. Again, make sure you check the admissions requirements and interview procedure of each individual school.

The On-Campus Interview

Plan the interview to coincide with a college visit. Even if you decide not to apply to the school, it's good practice. If the school is far away, this arrangement can also save money on travel costs.

If at all possible, schedule the interview for after your school tour. The next day is ideal, but if you're on a tight schedule, you can even arrange it for a few hours after you take the tour. This way you'll have intelligent

45

questions and answers for your interview. Weekdays are better than weekends for both an interview and a campus tour because lots more will be going on.

INTERNATIONAL COLLEGE COUNSELORS TIP: Go on your first interviews at your least favorite colleges. It's the best way to get practice.

The Alumni Interview

Different schools have different ways of arranging alumni interviews. Your chance of being asked to attend one really depends on how organized your area's alumni are and whether the school counts the interview.

The sooner you submit the application, the greater the chance of being offered an alumni interview. To increase the likelihood of being contacted for an interview, you should submit your application at least one month ahead of the deadline.

Each year, the first interview assignments are typically sent out to local alumni chapters in early September. Early decision applicants should expect to hear something about their interview by mid- November. Otherwise, the general rule is regular decision applicants may be contacted as late as mid-February/early March.

Whether you are called or not, may also depend on where you live. International students or students who live in remote areas may need to do an interview over the phone, via Skype, or skip it altogether. The best way to be sure is to call the school yourself and ask the admissions office how the alumni interview process works—and if it counts towards admission.

If the school gives you the name of the regional person who sets up the interviews, call or email that person. Then give your alumnus time to respond (five business days). These are volunteers who are often busy with career and family. If you still haven't received a response after five business days, contact the admissions office for a different alumnus on the list.

If your school of choice only offers informational interviews, you may need to be the one to initiate the process. Whether or not you are offered an interview may be more dependent on the enthusiasm and schedules of local alumni than whether the school is seriously considering you.

If the policy of the college is to contact the student and you don't get offered an informational interview, this may not be a reflection on you or your application. Many colleges, including some Ivies, have no prescreening process for interviews. They try to reach every applicant.

If you have not heard from a much-wanted school, you need to find out if you can request an interview. Some schools do not allow interview requests, while others, like Duke, do. Again, call the school admissions office or go online to see what the college policy is. If the school does allow you to request an interview, they will tell you what the next steps are.

If you've already been contacted by an alum for a mandatory evaluative (one that counts) interview, make sure you prepare, show up on time, and send a thank-you note.

Admissions offices know that not every applicant will be contacted for an interview, and they will not hold this against a candidacy.

IINTERNATIONAL COLLEGE COUNSELOR TIP: Students need to know the alumni interview policy of the colleges about which they are serious. Many universities have limited alumni who will interview, and so interviews are on a first-come, first-served basis. The earlier you send in your application, the better chance you have of getting an interview.

PREPARING FOR THE COLLEGE INTERVIEW: BEFORE THE INTERVIEW

Interviewers are looking for well-presented and well-researched honesty. Here's how you do that.

Outline the answers to questions the interviewer will most likely ask.

Some common interview questions include:

- Why do you want to attend this university?
- What do you know about our university?
- What do you want to get out of your college experience?
- What could you contribute to our college community?
- Is this school your first choice and why? o What other schools are you applying to?
- What major(s) are you interested in?
- What classes do you like the best at your high school and why?
- What extracurricular activities are you most involved in?
- What have you liked or disliked about your school? What would you change?
- What was your favorite job/internship/volunteer experience and why?
- What do you expect to be doing ten years from now?
- How have you been a leader or demonstrated leadership?
- What about you is unique?
- How would your friends describe you?
- What are your greatest strengths and weaknesses?
- Describe a difficult choice you had to make and how you

handled it.

- What has been your proudest life achievement so far?
- What book/film/television show has made the biggest impact on you?
- Who is the most influential person in your life?
- Is there anything else you want to add?

Some uncommon, but sometimes asked, college interview questions include:

- If you could be any animal, what would you be and why?
- What are three words that describe you?
- When do you feel proudest about yourself?
- If you could be any type of fruit, what would you be and why?
- What is your favorite color?
- If you could trade places with any other person for a week, famous or not famous, living or dead, real or fictional, with whom would it be?
- If Hollywood made a movie about your life, what actor or actress would play you?
- If you were a car, what kind of car would you be?
- What can our college offer you that another college can't?
- If you had a thousand dollars to give away, what would you do with it?

Do research!

Good answers require research. Do research on the college. Know why you want to attend. Know which programs and extracurricular activities you are interested in participating in and why. If there are faculty members of interest or graduates who inspire you, mention them.

Also prepare by thinking of examples where you have been successful. Make a list of your skills and interests as well as your strengths and weaknesses. Be familiar with your own resume.

Practice. Practice. Practice.

Practice will make you better (but you don't need to be perfect). Prepare answers to commonly asked interview questions. But, don't try to memorize them or you will probably come off as stilted, unnatural, and over-rehearsed.

Practice with a parent or a friend and videotape your session. Afterwards, replay the interview and see how well you did. Some specific things to consider include:

▸ Your responses. Are they clear and understandable or vague and uncertain?

▸ Your give-and-take. Are your answers too short or too long?

▸ Your engagement. Do you have a good handshake, good eye contact, a nice smile?

▸ Your speech. Are you talking too fast, too slow, too quiet, o r too loud? Do you say "um," "you know," or "like" too frequently?

▸ Your posture. Are you transmitting interest?

Pull together a list of thoughtful questions to ask the interviewer.

Good questions include: "What is the personality of this college as you've experienced it? What kind of student is happy here? What kind of student is not happy here? What are some of the best features of the school? Why did you choose to work here?"

Offer to send a resume to the interviewer before the interview.

By doing this, he or she can be more familiar with your accomplishments, and conversation will be easier for both of you.

WHAT TO WEAR TO A COLLEGE INTERVIEW

In addition to your good, well-thought-out answers, you need to winningly present yourself in dress and social skills. Spend time preparing your appearance and your presentation. An interviewee should look, not only sound, impressive. The big picture of any student for a school is that you will be a representative of them.

Wear the right clothes, as in "dress for success."
The key is to dress in a manner that suggests you are serious and taking the meeting seriously. It's about putting your best foot forward and showing respect, enthusiasm, and interest in a formal atmosphere. This being said, avoid jeans, shorts, tank tops, flip- flops, sandals, Crocs, or anything that's too tight, too short, too provocative, or too revealing.

Given that, you also need to feel comfortable and confident. For men, a safe list of clothes includes khakis, a light blue or white collared shirt, and a jacket. For ladies, a nice blouse, a long skirt or pants, and possibly a jacket. Showing a flash of your own style is nice as long as it doesn't include anything provocative or profane. And, please, clothes do need to be neat, not as if you fell out of bed and into yesterday's clothes.

Sure, you can always argue that if a college doesn't like the way you are, maybe the college isn't for you. Remind yourself that focusing too much on "being yourself" in an interview can take away from what is far more important to universities, and that is who you will become.

And if you do decide to wear a tank top and cut-off shorts and the interview goes sour and the college rejects you, then, yes, the college wasn't for you.

Of course, if you have a brilliant transcript, sterling SAT scores, and international recognition, those will trump even the scruffiest of looks.

Then again, here are some real deal-breakers that some college admissions officers swear they've seen. Students who:

- Arrive barefoot
- Obviously haven't showered in days
- Sit on the floor, rather than the chair provided
- Put their feet up on the couch, chair, desk, or coffee table
- Pick their noses (or at any part of their body) during the interview
- Swear during the interview
- Answer their cell phone and text
- Wear their earphones, sunglasses, or hats the entire time
- Bring along the family pet

DURING THE INTERVIEW

- During the interview, you want to be professional, engaging, positive, and enthusiastic at all times. Furthermore, and just as importantly:
- Smile.
- Look the interviewer in the eye.
- Show up to the interview on time. "On time" means ten to fifteen minutes early.
- Do not chew gum, eat, or slouch.
- Do not wear too much perfume or cologne.
- Turn off your cell phone. Not on vibrate. Off.
- Do not use generational slang or language that would be inappropriate in a business setting.
- Avoid giving " yes," " no," or one-word answers. In answering any question, you want to offer details. If you're asked what your favorite high school subject was, reply with more information than the one-word, "History." Did you prefer U.S., European, world, or state history? Explain what time period you liked best. Start a

conversation that almost every interviewer can enjoy.

- If the interviewer asks you what other colleges you are considering, don't be afraid to offer up a name or two. Do offer good, logical reasoning on why you like the interviewer's college better.

- At the end of the interview, leave the interviewer with two or three points you want him or her to remember you by. A good ending: " I am very passionate about astronomy, have done my homework on colleges, and know that this school is the best school for me."

- Before leaving, shake the interviewer's hand and thank him or her for the opportunity to meet.

- Endnote: Be who you are—but a little bit better, better dressed, and more well mannered.

WHAT TO REMEMBER FOR A COLLEGE INTERVIEW

Resumes
Bring two copies of your resume so you'll be ready if the interviewer asks you to share your experiences and accomplishments. The second copy is for the interviewer. See the end of this chapter for how to write a high school resume. Place the resume in a padfolio or large, clean manila envelope.

The Interviewer's Name
One of the top interviewing mistakes is not remembering the name of the interviewer. Make sure you remember with whom you are meeting.

The Interviewer's Phone Number
If for some reason you ran into an emergency or you are running late, you can attempt to contact the interviewer to tell of your situation.

The Interview Location's Name and Directions
You do not want to get lost.

Girls may bring a nice, simple purse while men may bring a nice, clean messenger-style bag.

WHAT <u>NOT</u> TO BRING TO A COLLEGE INTERVIEW

Your parents. Parents should never, ever sit in on the interview. Neither should siblings, cousins, friends, or dogs—unless it is a service dog, and even then you should ask ahead. There is a chance the interviewer may be allergic.

AFTER THE INTERVIEW

Follow up!
The impression you make does not end when the interview ends. Write a handwritten thank-you note after your interview to show you are a professional, polite person who values the interviewer's time. A thank-you note also offers the opportunity to reiterate key points you made during your interview.

A thank-you letter sent by snail mail within twenty-four hours of your interview will most likely get there within a day or two. These days, email works as well. You want the interviewer to know that you appreciate his or her time.

In your note, reference something in the interview that you talked about so it doesn't look like a generic thank-you note you send to everyone.

Here is a sample email/note:

Formal Interview Follow-Up

Dear Mr./Ms.,

Thank you for taking the time out of your busy schedule to meet with me. I enjoyed meeting with you and learning more about [NAME OF COLLEGE].

Per our conversation, I am extremely interested in attending [NAME OF COLLEGE]. I enjoyed hearing about why you chose to attend [NAME OF COLLEGE] and how it has helped make you the person that you are today. Your candor and passion have further solidified my desire to attend. I especially enjoyed learning about [Insert an interesting fact here that the interviewer told you].

I strongly believe that I will be a great fit at [NAME OF COLLEGE]. Thank you again for taking the time to meet with me and answering all my questions.

Sincerely,

[Your name]

POST THANK-YOU NOTE

If you tell the admissions counselor or alum you'll get in touch with him or her again, then you need to do it. We recommend you keep any follow-ups short and positive. Let the admissions office know of any new achievements. Don't send emails asking them for answers to questions you can find somewhere else, like on the college website.

HOW TO WRITE A HIGH SCHOOL RESUME

Writing a high school resume for college admissions is different from writing one for work. The best advice is to keep it simple. You want to create a concise and easy-to-read document that best presents your accomplishments. The college admissions teams will not be impressed with fancy type unless you're applying to art school.

Create a list.
Start with the 9th grade and make note of all activities, honors, memberships, and enrichment programs by quarter. Don't leave off summers.

Organize into major categories.
Next organize the information into major categories: honors, extracurricular activities, community service, sports, enrichment, special skills, and work experience. Sometimes, the information "buckets" are listed on college applications.

Organize into subcategories.
Organize the individual entries by category and date. Be specific about positions, titles, organizations, and locations. Do not use acronyms; for example, write out "Miami Beach Senior High School" instead of "MBSH."

Include special skills and certifications.
Make sure you include any special skills and certifications. They show accomplishment and offer an indication of deeper interest in an activity. For example, if you are in a swimming-instruction program, list your Red Cross Lifeguard certification. If you can speak more than one language, list them. If you practice taekwondo, add the belt level you've reached.

On the Common Application, you should add these skills to the Activities section.

Format the information.

Format the information on a document in a way you think is clear and attractive. On the top of the page, put your name, address, cell and home phone numbers, and email address. Ideally the resume will be one page long. Make sure it is no longer than two pages.

Sample Resume

Jordan Bloggs
501 Main Street; Miami, FL 33133
C: (305) 555-0000 – jbloggs@xyz.com

Education

Lincoln High School	Expected Graduation Date: [Month/Year]
Address	GPA:
Phone Number	SAT/ACT Scores:

Honors, Awards and Distinctions

Mu Alpha Theta (Math Honor Society)—VP 12, Member 11 Lincoln High Basketball Team—MVP & Captain 12

Lincoln High Honor Roll—9, 10, 11

Winner of the International College Counselors Essay Scholarship—11 Short story featured in *Teen Ink*—11

AP Scholar Award—11

Chatham University's Rachel Carson Book Award—11

National Honor Society—Member 11, 12

Sample Resume (continued)

Extracurricular Activities

International Club—Founder and President 11, 12

20 weeks per year, 2 hours per week

—Was selected to represent Lincoln High at the International Conference in California, 12.

Varsity Basketball Team—9, 10, 11, 12

35 weeks per year, 10 hours per week

—Played starting power forward for Lincoln High's basketball team. Averaged 8.4 points per game and 1.6 assists per game.

Mu Alpha Theta math tutor—11, 12

20 weeks per year, 2 hours per week

—Tutored students in Algebra and Algebra II.

Writer for *Eagles*, the school newspaper—11, 12

35 weeks per year, 2 hours per week

—Wrote monthly stories and articles about current events.

Chess Club—9, 10, 11

20 weeks per year, 1 hour per week

—Attended monthly meetings, competed in in-school chess matches.

Key Club Service Club—9, 10, 11, 12

25 weeks per year, 1 hour per week

—Organized food drives and participated in fundraising and charity events.

Sample Resume (continued)

Employment

Mt. Sinai Hospital—11, 12

25 weeks per year, 4–8 hours per week

—Interned in the Magnetic Resonance Imaging Department, learned how to use MRIs and evaluate images, explored the working experience of doctors.

Mr. C's Sports—10

25 weeks per year, 10 hours per week

—Worked as a salesperson, customer service representative, and cashier.

Summer Activities

Summer Journalism Institute at the University of Florida—12

—Was selected to attend a one-week intensive workshop in storytelling, editing, designing, photography, and multimedia.

Study-Abroad Program in Spain through Choate Rosemary Hall—11

—Participated in a five-week immersion program. Attended three courses taught in Spanish.

YMCA Basketball Camp Counselor—10 (8 weeks), 11 (4 weeks)

—Led a group of 7–12 year old children. Taught basketball skills, coordinated games, and counseled them during the summer.

Chapter 7:
Standardized Tests

L ike it or not, the SAT/ACT will most likely help to determine which colleges you will be able to attend. Don't discount the test as simply one of many factors that will be considered, or believe that it is not very important. The reality is that unless you are a professional- level athlete or a math whiz with a Nobel Prize, the SAT/ACT will likely play a major role in your college admissions.

It makes sense to get the highest score possible.

THE PSAT

You don't have to take this test. But you should.

The PSAT is the best practice for the SAT. It's a standardized test made by the College Board, the same company that creates the SAT, and it tests the same three subjects as the SAT: critical reading, math, and writing. The kinds of questions and the directions are almost exactly the same as the SAT. You get to experience sitting down for a two- to three-hour test with few breaks. For many, it's an eye-opener. The real SAT is about an hour and a half longer than the PSAT.

PSAT scores indicate how you might do on each section on the SAT. Using the test results, you can then focus your test review on the areas and types of questions you most need to improve. Scores can also be used as a gauge to see what kind of additional study aids or tutoring is needed. Consider poor results as an early warning signal that serious work may be needed before a student takes the real SAT.

By taking the PSAT, you could become a National Merit Scholar. This is a highly prestigious recognition. To participate in the National Merit Scholarship Program, a student needs to score above a certain percentile on the test.

Through the National Merit Scholarship Corporation (NMSC), different sponsor organizations offer different amounts of scholarship money to high-scoring students, even if the student reaches levels below that of National Merit Scholar.

High-scoring African-American high school students will become eligible to participate in the National Achievement Scholarship Program, as well as in the National Merit Scholarship Program.

Outstanding Hispanic/Latino high school students may be identified by the National Hispanic Recognition Program (NHRP).

By taking the PSAT, you can also see how your performance on the SAT test might compare with that of other students. This may boost self-esteem or be a good dose of reality/kick in the pants.

THE ACT PLAN

The ACT PLAN is similar to the PSAT, but prepares a student for the ACT. The test is offered to 10th graders. Not as many high schools offer the ACT PLAN as they do the PSAT. However, if your school offers the test, you should take it.

Similar to the ACT, the ACT PLAN covers English, Math, Reading, and Science. Taking the ACT PLAN will help students identify their strengths and areas where they need improvement.

THE ACT AND SAT

How early is too early to study for the SAT and ACT?

Freshmen and sophomores: It's not too early.

When should you start studying for the SAT and ACT?
  a. Now
  b. Immediately
  c. Forthwith
  d. All of the above.

Answer: d. For "duh"

It's never too early to start studying for the SAT or ACT. Do not plan on cramming for these critical tests. These tests are scored on a curve, and students are taking the tests worldwide.

Students who finish their exams in their junior year are always the happiest and usually the most successful.

Juniors: Take your standardized tests. Procrastination time is OVER. Juniors: FINISH all standardized tests THIS YEAR. This includes the ACT/ SAT/ TOEFL and SUBJECT TESTS.

Waiting until the fall is almost always a bad idea.

▸ It makes choosing an early decision school extremely difficult.

▸ Students cannot apply in August to rolling admissions schools.

▸ If an emergency arises on the day of the test, or you're sick, or your car breaks down, there will be no time to take the test again. If your dismal day happens on the last possible test date, you're truly out of luck—your bad score may be the one you'll have to live with.

Sure, college counselors will agree there's no point in taking a standardized test if you aren't ready, but most of you reading this now will have enough time to prepare.

For more details on the SAT and ACT tests, go online or take a look at all the resources out there. For SAT test prep, we highly recommend *The Official SAT Study Guide* by The College Board. For ACT test prep, we recommend *The Real ACT Prep Guide*. These are the only books we know of that feature official practice tests created by the test makers. The most recent edition will have the most up-to-date information.

How many times should I take the SAT and ACT?

This is the inevitable question. There is no magic number. But I will say that students should take the test AT LEAST two times, ideally more. Students fear that admissions officers will look at taking the test three or four times as too many and then penalize the student. This is not the case. I have never heard of a school rejecting a student for taking the test four times.

Even if they ask to see all scores, most schools will only consider the top scores. They pull the top ACT score and top SAT score in each of the categories, and that's it. So, if you're trying to get within a school's range, and you're off by a few hundred points in the SAT, it's definitely worth it to keep trying.

Of the schools that look at all the scores, usually admissions officers consider taking the test multiple times to be a sign of initiative, especially if you keep increasing your score. However, if you keep taking the test and you're doing poorer or plateauing, this is not a good thing. You need to regroup and consider tutoring or other study aids.

Each time you take the test, you should have studied and feel prepared that you're going to do well and increase your score from the previous time.

DIFFERENCES BETWEEN ACT AND SAT AND WHICH TO TAKE

Most colleges don't prefer one test over the other. The trick is to figure out which one is best suited to your standardized testing strengths. Each test emphasizes different test-taking skills and tests your familiarity in different subjects.

Here are some facts about the ACT and SAT:

The ACT

▸ Is designed to evaluate your overall educational development and your ability to complete college-level work.

▸ Has four multiple-choice subject tests covering English, Math, Reading, and Science. Each content area is approached in one big chunk, with the optional Writing Test at the end.

▸ Includes an optional 30-minute writing test designed to measure your skill in planning and writing a short essay. If you opt to take it, the additional scores will be listed separately.

▸ Has 215 questions.

▸ You'll have 2 hours and 55 minutes, not including breaks or the 30-minute optional essay. This makes the test faster paced.

▸ There is no penalty for incorrect answers; only correct responses count. So there is no penalty for guessing.

▸ Subject test scores (ranging from 1 to 36) are determined by correct answers. The four areas are then averaged together to come up with your overall, or composite, score.

▸ The ACT Math section requires you to have a broader range of knowledge than the SAT. For example, on this test there's a little trigonometry, in addition to algebra and geometry. That said, the ACT Math section is not necessarily harder, since many students find the questions to be more direct.

▸ Focuses more on grammar and punctuation.

▸ The science section tests logical reasoning based on data and scientific terms and is not based on classroom science.

▸ ACT Reading asks questions that rely more on retrieving information from the text.

▸ ACT questions are said to be more straightforward and easier to understand on a first read than those on the SAT. The ACT is also more intuitive and a better measure of what a student has learned in school.

64

The SAT

- Is designed to evaluate your general thinking and problem-solving abilities.

- Content areas (Critical Reading, Math, and Writing) are broken up into ten sections, with the required essay at the beginning. Keep in mind, this means you will be moving back and forth between different content areas.

- Includes a required 25-minute essay.

- Has 170 questions.

- You'll have 3 hours and 45 minutes to complete the test, with three short breaks.

- Test scores range from 600 to 2400, combining test results from three 800-point sections.

- Gives a slight penalty for wrong answers on the multiple choice questions.

- Unlike the ACT, the SAT has a part in the Math section where you'll be required to produce your answers.

- SAT Critical Reading relies more on prediction, inference, etc.

- Favors those who are very strong in vocabulary. If you aren't an ardent wordsmith, and if English is not your first language, you may do better on the ACT.

- The SAT is often described as a more teachable test. The "tricks" and "puzzles" can be learned because there are more test-specific concepts.

Almost all competitive colleges "cherry-pick" SAT sub-scores, meaning they consider the best combination of Math, Critical Reading, and Writing earned on different dates. Although increasing, fewer colleges do this with the four ACT sub-scores.

INTERNATIONAL COLLEGE COUNSELORS TIP: Take practice tests to see which test you prefer. As all colleges accept scores from both the SAT and ACT, consider taking both tests to see which one you perform better on.

THE ANTIDOTE TO BORING STUDY AIDS

What you may not realize is that there are many types of test prep materials available. Some are even fun. Check out all the options that exist.

Online you can find crosswords and other games. If you like to read, there are mystery books, vampire novels, classic literature paperbacks, vocabulary cartoons, manga comics, and a few potboilers designed to strengthen vocabulary. There are also the flash cards. If you are an audio learner, or so busy that shower time is your only free time to add another activity, there are rap songs and rock songs that have been written as SAT and ACT prep. There are also many phone apps available. Even on Twitter you can find SAT tutors offering a word a day.

There are a number of different books written to help students tackle the math sections of the SAT and ACT, too. Head to your local bookstore or hop online to find the books that most appeal to you. While the test is always the same, different authors take different approaches.

Google searches to find books or online study aids can include:

- SAT/ACT Vocabulary Novel
- SAT/ACT Vocabulary Games
- SAT Rap Songs
- TOFEL Rap Songs
- SAT Test Games
- Vocabulary Cartoons

- SAT Cookbook

On Twitter, look to follow names that include the following words:

- SAT
- ACT
- Vocabulary
- Tutor
- TestPrep
- GMAT
- GRE

KNOW YOUR SAT & ACT REPORTING RIGHTS

As many seniors will currently attest, some high schools are reporting on the high school transcript all college entrance scores provided by the testing agency, namely the College Board (SAT) and the American College Testing (ACT) programs.

Prior to sending your transcripts, you should look into whether your high school is doing this. At most schools, you do have the opportunity to decide if your scores will be recorded on your transcript. This will be done on an all-or-none basis.

If you do nothing, and your school has the capability to include scores, all scores (SAT, SAT Subject, and ACT tests) will be reported. If your choice is to not have your scores recorded on your transcript, you can take advantage of the College Board Score Choice option, or even choose to send no scores. Please note that some schools don't accept the School Choice option, so check with each school individually on its policy.

Regardless of which option you choose, understand that all schools and some scholarships require official score reports from the testing agency.

In this case, the official score must be sent from the College Board or the American College Testing program.

SAT SUBJECT TESTS

SAT Subject Tests Overview

Although less and less common, some schools—such as Harvard, Georgetown, and some top engineering programs—still like to see students take the SAT Subject Tests (formerly known as the SAT II and Achievement Tests). To them, these specific subject exams demonstrate your actual understanding of a subject area, meaning how well you have learned each subject and how prepared you will be for college-level courses.

Colleges like the SAT Subject Tests because, like all standardized tests, they make the admissions department's job easier. When tests are standardized, colleges can easily use them to compare you to other high school students nationwide.

You see, colleges are well aware that high school grades aren't always an accurate measurement of a student's ability. Some high schools are more difficult than others, some teachers are harder graders than others, and some students earn extra credit for random activities not available to all others. All of these possible factors leave equally talented students receiving different grades. Standardized tests are the great equalizer.

The tests include: Literature, U.S. History, World History, Mathematics Levels I and II, Biology, Chemistry, Physics, Chinese, French, German, Spanish, Modern Hebrew, Italian, Latin, Japanese, and Korean.

Not all schools require them, so you should check the universities' requirements before registering for any SAT Subject Tests. The scores range from 200–800, as in the SAT I.

Taking the SAT Subject Tests

Each exam is one hour in length. Prepare yourself like you would for the SAT. Get familiar with the format of the tests. Take old exams for practice if you can.

These tests aren't easy. The best time to take one of the SAT Subject Tests is right after you've finished a year-long course in that subject. This way the subject matter will still be fresh in your mind. Some exceptions would be if you plan to take the test in Foreign Language or Literature. Then you'd want to take the test after the highest-level class you plan to take. Also, if you prefer a language exam with listening, be sure to check the date it is offered (normally in October). Of course, there is no point in taking SAT Subject Tests after November of your senior year; everything should have been sent to the college admissions way before then. The only reason to take them this late would be if the colleges you're applying to use the SAT Subject Tests for placement or credit purposes.

The test dates for SAT Subject Tests are usually in October, November, December, January, May, and June. However, not every subject test is offered on each of the test dates. Note that you cannot take the SAT Subject Tests and the SAT on the same day, so you must plan your testing dates accordingly. To check when the tests you want to take are offered, refer to the College Board website at http://www.collegeboard.com.

INTERNATIONAL COLLEGE COUNSELORS TIP: You can take up to three Subject Tests on the same day, but it's not recommended. We recommend two exams to one sitting. Don't underestimate the difficulty of these exams.

What do the SAT Subject Test scores mean?
An average score varies widely from test to test. It's all about who is taking the tests and what scores they earn. Most often, students aiming for highly competitive schools take the test, because these are the schools that are asking for the scores.

What do the SAT Subject Test Scores mean to me?
The way to think about these scores is that they are part of your story. So, if you say you are fabulous at math, you should do well on the math

subject test. If you are just a "good" student with nothing really outstanding, these scores will likely support that.

TEST PREP COURSES

If you can take them, you should.

Some high schools provide SAT/ACT prep courses as part of their curricular offerings, and a variety of community-based organizations have free or discounted prep programs.

Private tutors and private prep programs can teach you strategies tailored towards your learning level and ability. Furthermore, they offer the flexibility and convenience to work around your schedule and provide you with fewer distractions than class settings.

NO SAT OR ACT SCORES REQUIRED

There are schools that don't use SAT or ACT scores for admitting students. Some of these schools only exempt students who meet certain GPA or class rank requirements. Other schools want to see your SAT or ACT scores, but only use them for placement purposes or to conduct research studies. If you are considering one of these schools, make sure you fully understand what the individual school's policy is. Admissions policies can and do change.

Here is a link to a list of SAT- and ACT-optional four-year colleges: http://www.fairtest.org/university/optional.

Chapter 8:
AP Courses and Tests

I f you're a strong student, you should take Advanced Placement (AP) courses.

Colleges like them, and they're good for you. Some schools offer International Baccalaureate (IB) courses, which are considered similar in rigor to AP courses. Both are good and show you've challenged yourself academically.

AP courses are designed to give you college-level courses in high school. Through AP exams, you can earn college credits and gain significant advantages in the college admissions process and on applying to scholarships. (See Chapter 18 on how they can even save you $$$$.)

Currently, there are over thirty AP courses to choose from, including Art History, Chemistry, Chinese Language and Culture, Computer Science, Environmental Science, Music Theory, and Psychology.

The final exam is reported on a scale of 1–5 (1 being the lowest and 5 being the highest) and shows how well you mastered the material.

Most four-year colleges in the United States give credit, accelerated placement, or both on the basis of AP Exam scores. By entering college with AP credits, you can save money on college courses and possibly graduate from college early.

Whether you get the college credits depends on your scores and on your college.

Most colleges will give college credit for a score of 3, but all colleges do set their own standards. Some schools also limit how many AP credits they will accept regardless of your score.

There is no right or wrong number of AP courses to take. These are looked at in context with the rest of your application.

If you are applying to the more competitive schools, I recommend that you take as many AP classes as you can handle.

TO REPORT THE AP TEST OR NOT TO REPORT THE AP TEST

After taking one of the many various AP tests, there are usually three ways a student will feel: Great! Good. And Awful.

If you think you did great or good, congratulations!

If you're sure you did awfully and scored a 1 or a 2, or you're not sure how you did but you have a queasy feeling in your stomach that makes you want to throw up, you can withhold or cancel your score.

Schools do not ask you to send official scores any longer with applications, so you are usually free to disclose—or not disclose—scores as desired. Of course, if you list that you took an AP class, but don't disclose a score, it is usually assumed you got a 1 or a 2. Naturally, if you did get a 1 or 2, I usually recommend leaving it off anyway.

Additionally, many public schools do not request AP scores on applications, so you don't need to worry there. They are requested on the Common Application, but not required.

Because AP grades are released in July, any request for changes in reporting must be received by June 15.

Note that it's not likely that any one AP grade you submit, no matter how low, will fatally wound you.

CANCELING AP GRADES

Canceling an AP grade permanently means you'll never, ever see the grade and it's deleted from your record forever.

However, colleges will likely know you took the test because the class still appears on your transcript.

The option to cancel a score helps a number of students. Some of those students took an AP course but found it didn't cover all the information on the test. (And this happens more than you'd think.) This option also encourages the risk-takers, the students who take an AP exam in a subject they might not have taken the class for. (They're the ones who study a lot on their own.)

To cancel a score, you must notify the College Board by sending them an AP Score Cancellation Form by mail or fax with your signature by the middle of June. (The date changes, so visit http://www.apscore.org for the most updated information.)

This service is free, but note that the grade report that you and your school receive will indicate that the grade has been canceled.

WITHHOLDING AP GRADES

Withholding a score means you may have one or more grades withheld from the colleges you indicated on your answer sheet. This gives you the chance to see your scores before the schools.

You may later release the grade to that college by sending the score via the AP Services online score-reporting system or sending a signed written request and a small fee.

INTERNATIONAL COLLEGE COUNSELORS TIP: Do not send your scores to any colleges in May. Wait until early July before releasing any of your AP scores to colleges.

As explained to me by an AP representative, you only get to send your scores to one school free; any others are $15. In other words, if you choose to withhold your scores from all the colleges until you see them, you're only "losing" $15. Many students can think of the $15 as "insurance." It's easy to see your scores and then send them in if you want to. Sending your scores to additional schools can be done by phone.

To withhold a score, you must notify AP Services by completing and sending the AP Score Withholding Form that can be found online by the middle of June. (The date changes slightly, so visit for the most updated information.)

The fee to withhold a score is $10 per score per college, which can be paid via check or credit card.

Note that unlike a canceled score, a request to withhold a grade does not permanently delete your grade. A withheld AP grade counts in your AP average and affects AP scholar designations. This means you can choose the scores that work to your advantage and feel confident to take some extra AP exams.

The best strategy is to get great scores and include them.

TAKE THE AP TEST WITHOUT TAKING AN AP COURSE

Very few public schools offer all the AP courses. Some schools don't offer AP courses at all. Some students find that the AP course they want can't fit into their schedule. What if you are in a rural environment?

There's no reason to panic.

Colleges understand that not everyone has access to AP courses.

The good news is: You can take any of the AP tests if you want to, whether you're homeschooled, at an unaccredited private school, or in a school or city with few options.

According to the College Board, hundreds of students participate through independent study. Some states even sponsor online AP courses. To find out if your state offers online AP, visit your state's department of education website.

If your school already offers AP courses:
Contact your school's AP Coordinator to register for any of the exams, whether your school offers the course or not. He or she will guide you through the registration process.

If you attend a school that does not offer AP:
Arrange to take the test at a participating school. The College Board recommends that students who want to take an AP exam without taking the course should call AP Services at (609) 771-7300 or (888) 225-5427 no later than March 1 to get the names and telephone numbers of local AP Coordinators. They ask that you prepare a list of the exams you plan to take before you call. Contact the AP Coordinators identified by AP Services no later than March 15.

You can find more information on the process at:
http://www.collegeboard.com/student/testing/ap/reg.html.

AP TEST PREPARATION

To prepare for the AP exams, use standard study books from trustworthy sources, like the Princeton Review and the College Board. It also doesn't hurt to find a tutor if you can.

Students without access to AP courses can consider courses offered by public institutions and private companies. Some universities, such as Stanford and the University of California offer online learning programs that include AP courses.

Also, as I mentioned before, some states sponsor online AP courses. To find out if your state offers online AP, visit your state's department of education website.

When researching your options, make sure that the AP course is approved by The College Board. The College Board has strict curriculum standards for AP courses. Also, you need to check with your high school to see if it will give you credit for taking the course.

Chapter 9:
Summer Opportunities

Make summer count.

Students who want to shine on their college applications must make the most of their summers. You don't need to build huts in Costa Rica, climb Mt. Everest, or cure cancer, but you do need to do something meaningful.

Below is a smattering of ideas on how you can maximize your summer:

Get a great summer job or internship.
Summer jobs and internships are great ways to show colleges and your parents that you are successfully maturing into a responsible adult. There are few better ways to earn a little respect and gain valuable real-world experience.

In a tight job market, your best bet may be an internship. If you are financially secure and can afford the loss of income, get over the fact you'll get paid very little or not at all; that's what "internship" means. You'll be rich in experience and resume fodder. Think of it as a summer course.

What you want to do is land an internship in a field you're interested in. This is your chance to try out a job before you choose to major in it. If you think you might like to try advertising, check with your local agencies to see what internship opportunities are available. If you want to be a lawyer, see if you can work in a law firm. An internship is also great way to secure yourself a recommendation and get your foot in the door for future networking.

Having an internship or job can also help you narrow down what you don't like.

Take a job as a salesperson, and maybe you'll find that you hate nothing more than having to deal with people. Work in an office, and perhaps you'll discover nothing but drudgery. Working with an architect or at a television station might strip away the glamorous façade of the career and show you what the day-to-day can really be like.

More information and tips on jobs and interviews can be found in Chapter 10.

Volunteer.

Contrary to popular belief, working for nothing can be profitable. You can make a difference, gain experience, and explore your interests. For example, if a career in medicine interests you, you could volunteer a few hours a week at a hospital or nursing home. Interested in animals? Volunteer at the local animal shelter. Feeling entrepreneurial? Start a non-profit of your own. The choices are endless, and all your hard work and time can pay off. Colleges and universities adore students who can demonstrate that they make the effort to help others. You may not be making money, but you can make friends and networking connections. You'll also be accruing valuable material for those application essays and increasing your chances of winning a scholarship. Then there's the bottom line: you will be doing good—a wonderful reason to volunteer in itself.

Take a virtual class or try dual enrollment.

Flush out your resume and explore something new. Virtual classes and dual enrollment programs offer you a chance to choose something you want to learn. Try out a course from a major you're interested in. Explore aeronautical science or 17th-century literature. One of the benefits of being a public school student is that while private schools have been known to reject dual enrollment credit, at most public schools taking a virtual class or participating in a dual enrollment program can be applied to replace classes or utilized to raise your GPA. (At most schools, dual enrollment credit is equal to AP credit, thereby raising your GPA!) Classes can also help save you time and money if you take classes that count both for high school credit as well as college credit.

Through the dual enrollment program, students can take classes at a local college free of charge and earn college credit. The college credit earned can be applied to most schools students eventually attend. This will save you the cost of the class.

Depending on your public school, if you enter college with credit, you may be able to reduce your course load per term or even graduate early.

Pre-College Summer Programs

At a pre-college summer program, you can grow your mind, strengthen your college application, and explore possible fields of study. You can get a chance to spend some time abroad or on a college campus. Pre-college summer programs also offer marvelous opportunities to make contacts with students, professors, and administrators for advice, guidance, and letters of recommendation.

Pre-college summer program offerings include art, computer science, engineering, physics, biomedical engineering, theater, and more. Actually, for any interest, there is likely a pre-college summer program. There are summer programs focused on community service, healthcare, language, cultural immersion . . . the list really goes on and on.

Programs generally range in length from one to six weeks. Some of these programs can even earn you college credit.

Some programs are highly competitive, and others are open to anyone who can pay the fee. Many of these programs are expensive, but some do offer scholarships. I generally recommend these programs to students who have a strong interest in a particular subject and have a family that can afford the program.

Dive into a language immersion program.

There are a number of programs both in the U.S. and abroad. Perfecting a second or third language is always worthwhile. The additional benefits of study-abroad programs are cultural immersion and a greater understanding of the world. However, due to the growing emphasis on a global education, colleges look more and more favorably on any language immersion programs.

Start a business.

Launching a business or collaborating on one can be a great learning experience that can provide students with valuable skills and income. The general recommendation is that students start a simple business with an immediate and obvious customer base. The goal is to generate a profit. Students with a passion for business who want to learn more about entrepreneurship may consider attending a program to help them get started. Nova Southeastern University, for example, offers one called the Entrepreneurship Summer Camp and Personal Enrichment (ESCAPE). Similar programs also exist around the country.

SUMMER IMPACT ON SCHOLARSHIPS

I will talk about this more in Chapter 19, but certain scholarships are available for students who show high interest in pursuing certain careers. By using the summer to take a qualified interest to a higher level, you may become eligible for these scholarships. Demonstrating long-term interest in certain volunteer work or organizations can also boost your scholarship chances. Taking classes at a local community college or school can show colleges a deep interest in a particular scholarly area that may make you eligible for school scholarships.

As you weigh your options, know that colleges are looking for experience that is helping to guide you toward your long-term goals.

Highly selective colleges can tell the difference between real experience and resume polishers. To maximize the impact of a summer program, internship, volunteer position, or job on your application, I recommend you choose one that is part of an overall plan. Make sure any summer activities you choose help frame you as a person who is passionate about a select number of subjects or services.

For example, if your focus throughout high school has been on art, spending time in Italy studying art makes sense. If you opt for a summer community service program, find a way to build on your experience when you return. If you helped supervise an art camp for young children in Guatemala and saw they needed more art supplies, start a fundraising organization or seek donations to send back.

Enjoy your summer—wisely!

Chapter 10:
Jobs and Internships

Summer jobs and internships (whether they're paid or not) are a great way to prepare for life after high school or for college. Your experience can help you develop the professional talents you'll need at almost any job. This is an opportunity to work with diverse people in a professional setting, hone your time management, increase your real-world problem-solving skills, learn to take orders, and make mistakes that won't kill your career. Jobs and internships are also excellent boosters of self-esteem and self-confidence. If you can succeed in one job, you can succeed in many more.

HOW TO FIND AN INTERNSHIP OR JOB

To find an internship or job, use a combination of strategies. Start looking early.

Start your internship/job search during winter break. Finding an internship/job may be as easy as searching the web—a number of them are posted on websites. Other opportunities may require more effort or creativity to find.

Know what interests you.
Begin with an idea of what you want to do. While you're not expected to commit to any specific field, colleges want to see that you've made an educated decision on your jobs or internships. Is there something you want to learn how to do, or somewhere you want to be in ten years? Start with your interests. This is your chance to try out a career. Do you think you want to major in business, psychology, or political science? Are you interested in computers, sports, or animals?

Take to the Internet.
Think about what kind of job you want then look up employers in your area who you think you'd want to work for. Check their websites. They may have an internship or job posted. If not, telephone or email them and inquire about summer jobs or internships. Be prepared to give a short talk on your skills, strengths, and motivation for working there.

81

Start with the front desk person and then do a search to see if the company has someone who can help you.

Network, network, and network some more.
Speak with family, friends, your family's friends, teachers, and high school advisors about what type of job or internship you want. Ask them if they have any connections in the field. Maybe they can help you connect with possible employers or know someone who can. You won't know until you ask, and it's OK to ask. Be sure to send a thank- you note to anyone who helps you. Express your appreciation for their time and expertise.

Join LinkedIn.
LinkedIn enables you to find people you know or want to know and connect with them. You can ask your connections about job opportunities, join groups, and find jobs. Make sure that if you contact someone you don't know that you send a brief explanation of who you are and why you want to connect.

Do it the old-fashioned way.
Fill out applications or drop off resumes at prospective employers and temporary employment agencies.

Be creative.
Email or call someone in a company whose work you admire. Flatter them and see if they may need a helper. The worst they can do is say "no." If the person you call says no, write them a short note thanking him or her for their time and giving them your contact information, but do not call again.

If you can't find the job you want, think about creating your own job.

Don't limit yourself.
A job or internship should be about learning, unless you really need the money. When you start considering unpaid internships or lower-paying jobs, you'll have more choices. If you're willing, and financially able, to work for free, you may be able to create your own position at a family

member's or friend's company. You may be able to get a job or an internship at a company you really want to work for if you're willing to work for free. The trade off for less—or no—pay should be invaluable work experience that helps build your resume.

Make your own luck.
You may get lucky on the first call, but most likely not. It's a numbers game, and the more people you call, the luckier you will get. Keep thinking positively, and don't give up. You may get the job after one call, or fifty. The biggest regret is not trying hard enough.

Stay safe.
Keep your parent, guardian or other responsible adult informed of you job and internship search. If you decide to apply for a position, especially one you find online, run it by an adult you trust. Never go for an interview without letting an adult know. (Even adults should tell other adults if they're going to meet a stranger.)

THE JOB OR INTERNSHIP INTERVIEW

Normally, interviewers of high school students aren't looking for previous work history or unique skills. They're looking to see if you're smart, on top of things, a good communicator, and a good fit for the company. Both your attitude and your appearance will affect your chances of getting the job you want.

Here are a few things to remember:

Dress the part.
When you head out for your interview, avoid looking too casual. That means no sandals, jeans, sunglasses, hats, or cutoffs. Even if you'll be scooping ice cream behind a counter, it helps to look professional for the interview. See Chapter 6 for tips on what to wear to an interview.

Do your research.
Before the interview, go online and learn everything you can about the business you'll be interviewing with, including its corporate mission (the

company's purpose and what it's trying to achieve), its products or services, and what customers are saying. Then use what you learn when answering the interviewer's questions.

Be polite and be professional.
Send a thank-you note after the interview.

HOW TO MAKE THE MOST OF YOUR SUMMER INTERNSHIP OR JOB

Turn your experience into resume gold.
Find an internship or a job in a field you're interested in. But even short of that, any job or internship can lead to golden opportunities. Volunteer for extra tasks and look for opportunities to take advantage of. To do this, the best first step is to prove that you're responsible and resourceful.

For example, if you're working in an ice cream shop and your boss needs to leave a few hours early, volunteer to be put in charge. If you're given the responsibility to lead, this counts on your resume as Management. If you're working in an advertising firm and think you might want to be a copywriter, ask for the current assignments. Write the ads then ask for feedback. Who knows, they may even love your ad so much, they'll run it.

Make connections.
Build up personal relationships. Find a mentor. After the summer is over, make sure to stay in touch with the people you met and connected with—and stay connected. It's never too early to start building your professional network. A professionally geared site like LinkedIn.com is a good place to keep in touch.

Develop your professional people skills.
Hone in on people you admire. Study the qualities you admire in them. Take notes on their dress and what character traits put them ahead. Then try to emulate those traits.

Work on your professionalism.
Do what you can to show the company you're the one they should be watching and giving the plum assignments to. Be professional, serious, and responsible. This should earn you more respect and responsibility. Be on time for work, meetings, conference calls, and team- building exercises. Even better—come early. Make sure you dress for success, too.

Be proactive.
If your job or internship appears to be a sea of repetitive tasks like making photocopies or coffee, don't complain. Ask to have a meeting with your supervisor to ask about new opportunities or projects. If there is a job you want to try, ask your supervisor if you can join the team, observe the meetings, or otherwise contribute in some way. You won't know unless you ask. Even if they say no, you will gain the respect and attention of your older colleagues. Interns and employees who identify their employer's needs and ask for new challenges demonstrate the initiative and motivation that companies want.

Ask questions.
Always remember that a summer job or internship is a learning experience for you. While your employer expects to get some work from you, you are expected to be interested in what's going on. So ask questions. This is your chance to get advice and learn.

Learn to take criticism gracefully.
No one likes to be criticized, but you're sure to encounter many negative opinions throughout your life and career. Criticism can help you. Follow up a negative assessment by asking for their thoughts on what you could have done better. Are there resources you don't know about? Is it true you need to be more detail-oriented? And then put that information to use. The best part about a summer job or internship is that you're not expected to know everything. Both you and your employer know that you are there to learn.

Learn about yourself.
You're there to watch and observe. Use this time to find out more

about yourself. See what kind of people you relate to and what kind of work you like to do. Compare yourself to people on the job who you admire. Do they have skills you lack or can work on acquiring?

Reset your expectations.

It's good to have personal goals, but sometimes realities don't match our expectations. Rather than dwell on negatives of the job or internship, seek out and embrace the opportunities offered. Chances are you won't be given that assignment that saves a client and makes you a star. But, that's not why you're there. You're there to learn, expand your horizons, and add to your resume.

Always, always stay enthusiastic and positive!

A JOB OR INTERNSHIP FROM THE COLLEGE'S POINT OF VIEW

A challenging and educational internship that gives you practical, real work experience can look as good on your college application as attending Harvard summer school.

The trend in the past couple of years for competitive college-bound students was doing volunteer work, the more exotic the better. But then, taking two weeks out of the summer to help malaria victims in East Africa started to become the norm on college applications.

Admission officers looked for something new to set students apart from one another. The result: many college applications now ask for your "paid employment" experiences.

Interesting as well, admissions officers at several elite schools say they are giving more credit to students who have real-world jobs and less to students who have taken on "meaningful" activities that say "resume padding" louder than passion. (For community service to really count you need to show a solid pattern of volunteer activity.)

I have worked with plenty of Ivy-bound students who have worked as cleaners, landscapers, and waiters. These jobs show commitment and the ability to work hard, and chances are Mom and Dad were not called in to get the job in the first place!

Now is the time to start thinking about the future, not just college, but beyond. As importantly as where do you want to go, you need to answer the question of what do you want to do. If you fall in love with agricultural science or primatology (look that SAT word up), going to Harvard probably won't help you.

So, roll up your sleeves and get some real-life work experience to demonstrate what you are interested in, passionate about, and involved in.

INTERNATIONAL COLLEGE COUNSELORS TIP: The trick to filling the employment section of your resume during high school is not to look for opportunities with a good brand name, but rather opportunities where you will have the chance to actually DO something.

Chapter 11:
Volunteering and Community Service

COMMUNITY SERVICE PROJECTS THAT MAKE AN IMPACT

There are many reasons to do volunteer work:

- It's a requirement for certain scholarships.
- It will put you in a better position to get scholarships.
- You may get high school credit and/or graduation recognition.
- Colleges have come to expect it.
- Volunteer work looks great on a college application.
- Volunteer work is great for college essays.
- You can explore different career options
- You're passionate about a cause.
- It feels good to do good.

You can find volunteer opportunities through clubs, school, religious institutions, family, friends, or on your own.

The Perfect Community Service Combo: Passion, Commitment, Dedication, and Initiative

The person who will get the most attention from the colleges is not the one who claims, "I volunteered 400 hours in one year." What will get the college admissions officer's attention is how you talk about what you did and what you can say.

Ideally you want to say something like, "I volunteered at an inner-city school where I started a therapeutic music program for low-income children, raised funds to support it, recruited and trained more volunteers, got the instruments donated, and gained the project community recognition in the local paper."

In the above statement, the student shows passion, leadership, commitment, dedication, and initiative.

Best of the best is if you earn a position of leadership with a title. Best of the best of the best is if you get public recognition for your service. Perhaps you can appear in your local or school paper or—best of the best of the best of the best—get a national publication to take notice of you. (It has been done; read up about press releases.)

You get bonus points from colleges for choosing a volunteer opportunity that is consistent with your educational or career goals. If you're interested in going to medical school, volunteer in a hospital or with children with disabilities. If you want to be a lawyer, try working on an environmental campaign. If you have good public relations skills, consider organizing fundraisers for good causes. If you like to cook, work at a soup kitchen. Find something you enjoy doing, and you'll have no trouble earning the hours.

Volunteer doing something you love, and it won't feel like work at all.

Of course, the worst of the worst is doing no volunteer work at all.

HOW TO ACHIEVE THAT PERFECT COMMUNITY SERVICE COMBO

Clock the time.

You can work 100 hours a year. You can work 1,000 hours a year. Interestingly, the quantity of hours you volunteer is not the most important factor. Colleges want to know WHY you volunteered, HOW you chose the assignment, and HOW you handled your responsibilities.

Hours are important for you to show a pattern of consistency. (On many applications, you must write hours per week/weeks per year.) And it is important to be consistent.

Demonstrate focus.

It's better to be really involved in one or two volunteer activities than just do a few hours here and there or spend your time on lots of little meaningless projects.

If you spent a short period of time helping out with a project abroad, you need to turn that experience into a long-term mission once you return home. Unless you plan on going into Latin American Studies or Construction Management, colleges prefer you spend four years helping at a local shelter than spending a month building houses in Guatemala.

The ultimate goal is for you to become part of something important and show that you made an impact. A college wants to know that you found a focus and stuck with it.

Think creatively.

Think about ways you can expand on your community service. Come up with a goal of your own. If you are tutoring kids, make it a project to recruit more tutors. If you're working with the elderly, see if you can get a group of students to go to a nursing center once a month and entertain the residents. If you work with rescue animals, make it a mission to make cute videos encouraging people to adopt.

Areas of Community Service to Consider (with examples)

- Children (Do volunteer work for the YMCA or Girl Scouts.)

- Animals (Work at an animal rescue.)

- Elderly (Aid in a nursing home.)

- Tutoring (Assist middle school students with their homework.)

- Office work (Do social media work for a nonprofit group.)

- Environment (Clean a community park.)

- Hunger, housing, and homelessness (Serve food at a homeless shelter.)

- Medical (Participate in a hospital volunteer program.)

- Computer science (Create a website or community forum for a nonprofit.)
- Retail (Work at a local Salvation Army or Goodwill thrift store.)

The Service Trip Trap

Many companies offer exotic international trips with community service attachments. Before paying the thousands of dollars to attend, know that admissions officers are no longer that impressed with these trips. More and more students have been traveling abroad to fulfill community service requirements, and it is no longer seen as a unique accomplishment. If you do go on one of these trips, make sure you also volunteer locally and find a way to expand on your experience. No matter where you do your community service, the main importance is to demonstrate focus, commitment, dedication, and initiative.

Of course, if you have the opportunity to go, can afford the trip, and know you will have to do more volunteer work at home, go. It's a great experience. For students who can't afford the program cost, which typically runs $5,000 to $7,000 and more, some programs offer financial aid and outreach programs.

IF YOU CAN'T VOLUNTEER

There are exceptions to every "rule." If you truly can't afford to volunteer since you may need to watch a younger sibling or work to help support your family, make sure you explain this situation in your essay or in the "additional information" section on the application. If you explain your economic situation and how you are helping your family out, a number of admissions officers will consider this a form of service.

INTERNATIONAL COLLEGE COUNSELORS TIP: When describing your volunteer work/community service in your college admissions essays, make sure that you let the reader know what your experiences have taught you.

Chapter 12:
College Visits and Information Sessions

It's never too early to start looking at colleges, and there's no better way to learn more about a college than to check it out for yourself.

Sophomores or juniors in high school should start as soon as possible.

COLLEGE CAMPUS VISITS

Visiting the college is an important part of your college decision process. It is one thing to read about a school, but quite another to visit it. Visiting a school gives you a chance to ask questions, take a tour, sit in on classes, and obtain an overall perspective of the college's atmosphere. Going around to the different colleges will give you a chance to compare them and gain a better sense of which college is right for you.

On a campus visit, you'll see much, much more than you can see in a brochure or online. College marketing doesn't typically show the campus when it's buried under ten feet of snow.

How should I prepare for the visit?
You should definitely do a little research on the college before you visit. Start by looking through the brochures and on the college's website. On the tour, you can then ask questions about the things you're interested in knowing more about.

Make sure you visit the school's website to schedule a campus tour and information session at least two weeks before you plan to go. If you are a senior, consider scheduling an interview. But make sure you are very familiar with the school and have done some interview preparation before deciding to do so. (See Chapter 6 for interview preparation.)

When is the best time to visit a campus?
You'll get the best school experience when school is in session during the regular academic year. You'll be able to see and meet students and get a feel for the rhythm of the campus. You may even get a chance to

sit in on a class. On the flip side, if you visit the school while it is not in session, you'll find yourself touring a deserted campus.

Call the college or check out a school's academic calendar to find out when breaks, holidays, and exam periods are scheduled. You don't want to show up when no one is around or tours are not being given.

Mondays through Thursdays are the best days for visits. On Fridays, faculty and students are focusing more on the weekend ahead.

High schools and colleges are on different schedules, so there may be good opportunities for you to visit on holidays that fall on weekdays and during spring break. Many colleges begin their fall semester in mid-August, so also consider visiting in late summer and early September, before your high school semester begins.

You can also visit schools after you've been accepted. Many colleges invite accepted candidates to spend time on campus to encourage them to enroll. However, procrastinating this long won't give you much time for visits.

What should I bring along?
Comfortable walking shoes are a must since the tour should include a walk around the campus. You'll also want to bring a pen and a notebook to write down any notes that will help you remember the school. Pack a camera or video camera as well. Pictures will help you remember more details.

Who should I talk to?
Talk with as many people as you can. This list can include professors, admissions officers, and students. The best way to see the campus is to go on an official campus tour run through the admission office.

Admissions officers can give you answers about application deadlines, timing, and what the school is generally looking for in a student. Professors can give you a feel of what they expect—and all professors are different, so try to talk to as many as you can. Some schools even offer the opportunity to sit in on some of their classes. Look to students to give you the real scoop about the college as a whole. Since students are not employed by the college, they will usually give you the most honest answers.

INTERNATIONAL COLLEGE COUNSELORS TIP: If you plan to have an admission interview, or want to meet with a particular professor or financial aid officer, make an appointment. Call the school to arrange this before you make the pilgrimage.

What questions should I ask?
You should ask all the questions you need to get the information you want. We do recommend, however, staying away from asking the tour guide for statistics about the school that you can find on the website or in the catalog. We also don't recommend that you ask the admissions representatives all about the social life. Save that for any students you meet. We've provided some questions on the next page that you can use as a starting point.

Any last thoughts?
Yes. Be sure to "sign in" with legible handwriting. This will let the school know you were there and demonstrated interest by visiting. This will also give you good conversation for any admissions interviews. If you visit a school, make sure you mention it at some time during the interview.

Don't miss the opportunity to check out the local community. You'll want to know if the size of the town is right for you and if there's ample entertainment available, among other things.

Also, when you're back at home after your visit, don't forget to send thank-you notes or a thank-you email within forty-eight hours. Make sure to remember your guide's name, any interviewers you met with, and the professors you had a chance to talk to. This will put your name in their minds, and little things like this can make a difference.

College Visit Follow-Up

Dear Mr./Ms.,

I visited [NAME OF COLLEGE] on [date of visit]. [If you asked questions] I wanted to thank you for taking the time to talk to me and answer my questions.

[If you did not get a chance to ask a question] It was a pleasure meeting you. I had one quick follow-up question that I hoped you'd be able to answer. [Insert question here]

After visiting the school, exploring the campus, and meeting with you, my dream of attending [NAME OF COLLEGE] has been solidified. Thank you again for your help. I look forward to applying to [NAME OF COLLEGE].
Sincerely,

[Your name and High School]

COLLEGE TOUR, INFORMATION SESSION, AND INFORMATIONAL MEETING SAMPLE QUESTIONS

Academic Qs

- Are professors accessible outside of class?
- What is the typical way to get in touch with a professor? Email?
- Phone call?
- Do you usually get in all the classes that you need to register for?
- How many courses are taught by professors, and how many by a teaching assistant?
- What are the most popular majors? The least popular majors?
- What is the grading system like?

95

▶ What is the study-abroad program here like?

Financial Qs

▶ If you have financial need, will you be able to get a financial aid package that meets all of your demonstrated need?

▶ Are there work-study jobs available on campus? Off campus?

▶ If you don't qualify for work-study, what jobs are available near campus that you could apply for?

Safety Qs

▶ How safe is the campus? How often are crimes reported?

▶ Is the campus well lit?

▶ How large is the campus security force? Does it patrol campus regularly?

▶ Is there a pick-up or shuttle service for students walking at night?

▶ How late does it run?

▶ What services are offered by the campus health center? How large is it?

Campus Qs

▶ Does the campus seem too big? Or too small?

▶ Does the campus look well cared for?

▶ Do you feel comfortable and safe?

▶ Do most of the students seem to be like you, or are they completely different?

▶ Are you required to live on campus your first year?

▶ Are the dorms single sex or coed?

▶ Do freshmen live in their own dorms?

- Are the dorms quiet or noisy? Do they seem crowded?

- What are the rules for students living in dorms?

- What types of meal plans are available?

- What hours are food services available?

Social Qs

- What do students do on weekends? Stay on campus? Go home?

- What are the most popular extracurricular activities?

- What are the biggest student hangouts in and around campus?

- Are there sororities and fraternities on campus? How many students participate?

- Are parties allowed on campus?

Athletic Qs

- Is the college considered an athletic school?

- What sports are the most popular?

- Do athletes have to miss a lot of classes in order to participate in games?

- Do athletes have their own dorms?

- What's the condition of the laying fields and the sports equipment?

Qs for students

- Why did you choose this particular college?

- What's your least favorite thing about the school?

- Are professors helpful and accessible?

- What do you do on a typical weekend?

- If you had to do it over again, would you still choose to attend?

Community Qs

▸ Do you like the surrounding city or town?

▸ Is the city or town big enough for your taste? Does it have enough entertainment for you?

▸ How easy is it to get to places off campus? Will you need a car?

▸ Are there places within walking distance?

▸ What is the city's public transportation system like?

ATTENDING INFORMATION SESSIONS

Attending info sessions can help you learn about colleges and, as importantly, will enable colleges to learn about your interest.

College Campus Information Sessions

At a campus info session, representatives from a university will present information about their institution and answer questions about the college admissions process. Students, and parents who accompany them, will learn what distinguishes one school from another, what colleges look for in the selection process, and what one can do to enhance the college application. You'll also gain insights into campus life, financial aid, and the scholarship process. And there is always a Question and Answer period at the end. Generally, each session lasts approximately an hour. Current students and/or alumni may attend depending on where and when the information session is held. Sometimes food is served, and sometimes it's not.

Almost every school offers information sessions on campus. Call a school or check its website to see the schedule.

For Students Unable to Visit Universities

If money and time is an issue, don't feel as though you must visit a college in order to get in. University representatives travel around the U.S. and the world reaching out to students.

Finding out about upcoming college information sessions or college fairs where a college representative will be present and getting invited to them is as easy as going to a school's website and signing up on the admissions page to learn more. Almost every school has a "contact me for more information," page and it's the best way to stay on a college's radar.

College Representatives' Visits to High Schools

In many cases, college informational meetings can also take place at your public high school. A college's representative visits the high school, and students may be invited or can ask to attend. Ask to attend the representative visits for the schools that interest you. This is a great way to get to know a college and demonstrate interest to the admissions staff.

Schools let their students know about these visits in different ways. Some post notices near the guidance counselor office. Others post them on a website. Make sure you know how your school is letting people know which college reps are visiting and when, and check back often.

Be sure to fill out the contact form a representative is likely to hand out.

If a school representative comes to your high school and you don't bother to attend the meeting, an admissions officer might conclude that you are not that interested in the school. This is a big oops.

After the school representative's visit to your school, send a thank-you note or email within forty-eight hours after your visit. Here is a sample letter, but make sure to personalize and customize it with your information.

99

Informational Meeting Follow-Up

> *Dear Mr./Ms.,*
>
> *Thank you very much for visiting [NAME OF YOUR HIGH SCHOOL] on [date of visit]. I learned a lot about [NAME OF COLLEGE]. I was particularly impressed when you mentioned [Insert interesting fact here that the representative shared. For example, a new fitness center, an additional program in sports management, the diverse population, etc.].*
>
> *I appreciate you coming to talk to us. I look forward to applying to [NAME OF COLLEGE].*
>
> *Sincerely,*
>
> *[Your name]*

College Fairs

National college fairs span the U.S. from coast to coast and visit every major metropolitan area across the country. You won't find any Ferris wheels or cotton candy at these events, but you will find them to be outstanding opportunities to learn about a wide variety of schools. At a college fair you can attend helpful seminars, meet school representatives, and collect information on:

▸ Admission requirements

▸ Financial aid

▸ College majors and courses

▸ Admission requirements

▸ Life on campus

Generally, each school will have a table or booth stocked with informational brochures. A representative will often be there to answer any questions you may have about the college. Some college fairs are even attended by actual admissions officers—whom you can talk to! You can also pick up a lot of pens, bags, and other giveaway items.

Fairs are designed to help you cross some colleges off your list and discover new ones to add.

The majority of college fairs happen to be free and open to the public. International students and those who are unable to travel to the college fair locations should consider attending virtual college fairs. One of the most popular hosts for this is College Week Live. You can see their offerings at http://www.collegeweeklive.com.

To find more college fairs, use the search engine phrase: "college fair."

INTERNATIONAL COLLEGE COUNSELORS TIP: After meeting anyone connected to a college of interest, give them your contact information and ask them for a business card. If you meet a college representative virtually, ask them for contact information. It will show that you're interested in the university. It will also give you contact information, which is useful for follow-up questions and thank- you notes.

Below is a sample thank-you note/email that is clear, concise, and appreciative.

College Fair Visit Follow-Up

Dear Mr./Ms.,

I attended the [NAME OF COLLEGE FAIR] on [date of visit]. [If you asked questions] I wanted to thank you for taking the time to talk to me and answer my questions.

[If you did not get a chance to ask a question] It was a pleasure meeting you. I had one quick follow-up question that I hoped you'd be able to answer. [Insert question here.]

Thank you again for your help, and I look forward to applying to [NAME OF COLLEGE].

Sincerely,

[Your name and high school]

VIRTUAL TOURS

A number of schools offer video tours of campus. Others stream live webcams onto their websites, offer photorealistic tours, and have interactive campus maps online.

I think they're fun and another tool for students to use, but they're not a replacement for actual campus visits.

What virtual tours are especially good for is helping to weed out colleges you're kinda sorta interested in. They're also really helpful for international students and for students with difficulty traveling.

For virtual tours, take a look at

- CampusTours: http://www.campustours.com
- eCampusTours: http://www.ecampustours.com
- YOUniversityTV: http://www.youuniversitytv.com

Also visit a college's website and see if they offer one.

Chapter 13:
Choosing a College List

Choosing a college list is a really big decision, and up to this point in your life, you've probably never had to make a decision as big as this one.

You're not alone. There are thousands and thousands and thousands of public high school students around the world feeling as anxious as you are.

The trick is to make the process as least stressful as possible.

Knowledge is power, and the more you know about different colleges, the easier it will be to find the right college fit for you. What's good for one student isn't necessarily the best for another. You're not "competing" against anyone but yourself.

Dream big, but be open to compromise. You may be pleasantly surprised.

At International College Counselors, we are very concerned about "fit." I remember talking to a student who transferred from Duke because he simply did not like to watch basketball. And, while he appreciated his school's academics and spirit, so much of the social life revolved around basketball that he often felt like an outsider. Clearly, the fit of this school was not for him.

STEP ONE: DO A PRELIMINARY COLLEGE SEARCH

Hop on the Internet.
Familiarize yourself with what's out there. Get on your computer and start looking at college websites. Is there a college you've heard of that sounded interesting? Take a look at the website. Type the word "college" into a search engine and pick a city. See what comes up. Type in "college" with different words, like "warm weather," "geekiest," "friendliest," or "clown." If something looks interesting, take a deeper look. Did a friend, parent, teacher, or coach mention a college to you in

passing? Look it up.

Enhance your search by visiting college search web sites.
Princeton Review: http://www.princetonreview.com
Kaplan: http://www.kaplan.com
College Board: http://www.collegeboard.com

Take a look at websites for college rankings.
Website URLs are listed later in this chapter, but make sure to read my thoughts on college rankings.

Check out college guides.
These may be available at your high school or local library. You can also find them at bookstores and online at Amazon.com.

Take advantage of the college visits at your high school.
See Chapter 12 for more info on college visits.

Attend college information sessions.
See Chapter 12 for more info on college information sessions.

Attend college fairs in your area.
See Chapter 12 for more info on college fairs.

Ask around.
Talk to people you respect. Find out where they went to college and what it meant to them. Do you have a dream job? Ask Human Resources Directors where they recruit.

STEP TWO: MAKE A LIST OF WHAT YOUR COLLEGE MUST HAVE

Write down the top five things your college must have. These are the deal-breakers. If a college doesn't have these five things, you're going to cross it off your list. I would highly recommend one of those deal-breakers be your choice of major. If robotics is a career you're interested in, it's going to be very hard to explore the possibilities if the school has no resources for you to work with.

Make another list of the five things "I wish the college has." This list will help you weed down your list, but don't use it to cross schools off the list—yet. If an extracurricular you really want is not offered at a school, don't cross the college off the list. Open the door for opportunity. This may be a chance for you to start an organization at your college. College is the ideal time to explore leadership opportunities.

STEP THREE: DO IN-DEPTH RESEARCH

Hop online again.
If you're interested in a college, scour its official website. All colleges have one. Think of yourself as a detective, and look beyond the obvious facts like campus size, location, courses of study, and degree programs. Investigate campus activities, study-abroad programs, student organizations, special programs, etc.

Think about what you want.
College experiences differ greatly. A name brand isn't necessarily going to make a school the right fit for you. A better place to start is by considering academics, campus life, location, student profile, and financial aid. You will need to do some research to answer some of the following questions. Answers can be found online or by calling/emailing the school. Then it's up to you to decide how you feel about what you learn.

Sample questions to answer during your research:

Academic Qs

- Is there a program in my field? How strong is it?

- What classes are offered?

- Who is teaching in my area of study?

- How many students are in classes?

- What have graduates of the program gone on to do?

- What kind of real-life opportunities might be available to me as a student in this program (hands-on activities, internships, volunteer work, opportunities to meet potential employers)?

- Can I study abroad?

Campus Life Qs

- What kinds of activities are available?

- What are the sports options?

- What's the atmosphere like on campus?

- How important are fraternities and sororities?

- How safe is the campus?

- What kinds of student services are offered?

- What resources are available to help students succeed?

- Do I feel like I will fit in?

- Does the school meet my special needs? (For information on special needs see Chapter 14.)

School Size and Location Qs

- How many students are at the school?

- Is it a city campus, a rural campus, or a college- town campus?

- What is the typical weather?

- How far is it from home?

- What is the cost to travel home on holidays and weekends? How much time will the trip take?

School Profile Qs

- Does the college have a diverse student population?

- What is the SAT/ACT range?

- Are my scores above or below these numbers?

- What is the average GPA?

- Is my GPA comparable?

Financial Aid Qs

- What kind of financial aid is available?

- How will the amount of financial aid I receive be determined?

- What grants and scholarships are available, not just loans?

- How do I apply?

- When are the deadlines?

- What's the tuition?

- What might other costs be of attending? (Housing, books, meal plans, etc.)

- Are there resources available to help with these costs?

- What work opportunities are available, on or off campus?

- Can I work and attend classes?

- What is the difference between in-state and out-of-state tuition?

- What scholarships are available? How do I apply? When are the deadlines?

Do not cross off any colleges because of cost. Many colleges offer financial aid, scholarships, and other help that make them far more affordable than they first appear. I discuss financial aid in depth in Chapter 18.

STEP FOUR: GET A SECOND/THIRD/FOURTH/ETC. OPINION

Talk to alumni.
On most college websites, you can find information on the alumni association. If there are email addresses of alumni listed, send one email per alum asking if he or she would be open to speaking with you or answering a few questions. Do not assume that anyone will be able to talk immediately, or even want to talk. It is important to ask politely and set up a time to talk.

Be creative. Search the Internet for college-specific phrases in quotes, like, "I graduated from Muhlenberg," or "Since graduating from OSU." See what former and current students have to say.

Check out ranking sites where the rankings are based on student reviews:

▸ Student Review: http://www.studentsreview.com

▸ Rate my Professors: http://www.ratemyprofessors.com

Talk to your College Counselor.
He or she could give you additional advice and guidance as it applies to your school.

Talk with family, friends, teachers, and mentors.
These are trusted adults whom know you well.

Do a reality check.
Compare your academic profile to the profile of the most recently enrolled class for the colleges you are looking into. Some college websites have this information. Contact the school if you can't find it. This will give you a realistic understanding of what your chances are for getting into a school.

After comparing your test scores and grades, look at your list again. If your grades and scores are lower than the middle range scores of more than four schools on your list, you need to add more schools to your list.

My recommendation is to investigate at least three or four colleges that are not familiar to you. Basic requirements: Each one must offer the field of study that interests you, be appropriately selective for a student with your grades and scores, have a price or financial aid possibilities that you can afford, and have a location where you could happily live.

You may find that what you don't know now becomes all you dream about later.

STEP FIVE: VISIT SCHOOLS

If you can, visit at least three schools before your senior year starts. The Internet is no substitute for an actual college visit. If at all possible, sit in on a class. See more on college visits in Chapter 12.

STEP SIX: CREATE A COLLEGE LIST

Begin your senior year with a list of eight to ten colleges that interest you.

Don't believe you will only be happy at one school in the world. Oftentimes students "compromise" and go to schools that are not their first choice. Many of these students end up absolutely loving that school, staying there, and feeling quite lucky they didn't go anywhere else. Other students attend another school for one or two years and then transfer. For more on transferring, see Chapter 17.

Safety and Reach Schools

Every student's final college lists should have one or two safety schools on it. These are colleges to which you are almost absolutely certain you will be admitted. As importantly, there shouldn't be any schools on your list that you wouldn't be happy to attend.

Reach for your dreams and apply to a few "reach schools." If you're in the competitive zone or you play the bassoon and the school just happens to be looking for a bassoon player, you just may be in for a happy surprise.

U.S. News & World Report College Rankings and Their Meaning

College rankings lists are often considered a "must read" for most students and their families.

Some of the more well-known rankings lists come from:

- U.S. News & World Report: http://colleges.usnews.rankingsandreviews.com/college

- Businessweek (Business schools only): http://www.businessweek.com/bschools/undergrad

- The Princeton Review: http://www.princetonreview.com/college/college-rankings.aspx

- Kiplinger's: http://www.kiplinger.com/tools/colleges

- Forbes: http://www.forbes.com/top-colleges/list

- College Prowler: http://collegeprowler.com/rankings

Each organization and publication bases its ranking on multiple statistical measuring sticks, each weighted differently, and spread across different major categories.

Parents and students have been using these lists as a way to sort out schools.

Of course, as soon as rankings come out, colleges see them too. And the forces there begin strategizing about how they might raise their college up in the ranks in the next issue. Unsurprisingly, several colleges have been caught climbing the rankings by reinterpreting the meanings of rules, manipulating data, or just flat-out lying.

In my opinion, college rankings are nothing more than relying on the Miss America pageant to measure beauty. The only way to truly rank colleges is to consider what the value is to you. Rankings are useful in that they give you information to consider and weigh.

Working with the 'Rents

Communication is key for families going through the admissions process. Make sure you have a talk with your parents or guardians as you begin to choose your colleges. You need to understand what their thoughts are on the colleges and college locations you're considering. You should also gather their thoughts on your choice of major, financial aid, and, importantly, cost. Be open to listening to them. Be prepared to answer any questions they may have, as well. If you've chosen Celtic language as a possible major, explain to your parents why you chose it and what you plan to do with the degree. If you want to go to college across the country and they ask you why, good answers don't include the phrases "sun tanning" or "powder skiing." Another good move is to let your parents know that you plan to apply for scholarships and do what you can to help out with this significant financial investment.

If your parents insist you apply to a certain college, do it; don't fight it. It won't hurt, and until all the envelopes are in, you don't have to make any commitments.

If you really want to make your parents feel comfortable, schedule time at least once every two weeks to update them with what you're doing. Let them know about your test prep, school research, school counselor meetings, and scholarship applications. The more mature you can show them you are, the more trust you can earn.

Chapter 14:
Schools and Programs for Students with Learning Disabilities

There are support services available for students with learning disabilities. These services vary in quality and extent from school to school.

As more and more high school students with disabilities are applying to colleges, the schools are prepared to answer questions and provide guidance.

HOW TO CHOOSE A SCHOOL: AN OVERVIEW

Students with disabilities should follow the same steps for choosing and applying to a school as any other student. The more information you have, the more "educated" your decision can be. If you're a student with a disability, you need to evaluate schools based on their ability to accommodate your needs.

Good starting resources for students with disabilities who are applying to college include the Learning Disabilities Association of America (http://ldanatl.org) and the *K&W Guide to Colleges for Students with Learning Disabilities* by Marybeth Kravets. This 800+ page book profiles over 300 schools and includes information on services at each college, admissions requirements, and contact information for program administrators.

Start by reviewing your needs.
Sit down with knowledgeable adults—whether they are your parents, your Individual Education Plan (IEP) team, or your college admissions counselor—and start by reviewing your needs. The goal is to better understand your disability and its effect on your college choices. Ask these questions:

▸ How does my disability affect how I learn?

▸ What are my academic strengths?

- How do I learn best?

- What strategies do I need to help me learn?

- What facilities may I need?

- What environmental conditions do I need? (For example, if you are in a wheelchair, the best college for you may not be on a rural campus where it snows a lot.)

- What careers am I interested in? (Stay realistic about how any learning or physical needs may influence these career areas.)

Once you have these questions answered, begin building a college list. Once you narrow your college choices, contact the disability services office of each school to determine if a college has the services and accommodations that can support your needs and meet your specific requirements. Programs, policies, procedures, and facilities must meet the needs of your individual situation.

INVESTIGATE THE SCHOOLS

Most colleges have an office that provides services to students with disabilities, or a person who coordinates these services. This resource can usually be found at a school's counseling center or as part of student services. This office may be referred to by a number of names including the Office of Student Disability Services, Disability Support, Office of Disabled Student Services, and Learning Support Services.

Depending on your disability, here are some questions to ask the disability services representative:

- What documentation must I bring to identify myself as a student with a disability entitled to reasonable accommodation? How current must it be?

- How is confidential information handled?

- Who decides if I qualify for accommodations?

- Are the accommodations I need available?

▶ How much advance notice is needed to have textbooks recorded on tape?

▶ Is tutoring provided? What is the cost?

▶ Are waivers or substitutions granted to students who, because of their disabilities, cannot pass certain courses, such as foreign languages or statistics?

▶ Are basic skills, study skills, time management, or organizing classes offered? Are they available for credit? Can they be counted as hours toward full-time status? What is the cost?

▶ Is there a support group on campus for students with disabilities?

▶ Is there adaptive technology available?

▶ How many students does the support program serve?

▶ How many disability specialists work with the program full time and part time?

▶ Are disability specialists available for ongoing counseling, guidance and, support?

▶ Does the school offer specialized academic advising for students with disabilities?

▶ Does disability support help to communicate each student's needs to the appropriate professors?

▶ Is there a physician at student health who has experience treating and prescribing medication for my condition?

▶ Does the office have a listing of professionals in the area who are experienced in treating my condition?

I also recommend you visit each school's website for college disability services to get an idea of eligibility requirements, resources, services and accommodations, documentation required, available academic support, and policies.

You may also want to ask to meet with one or two other students with disabilities enrolled in the school who currently receive support services. They are often the best resource for practical information about the strengths and weaknesses of the program.

HOW TO MAKE YOURSELF A STRONG CANDIDATE FOR ADMISSIONS

Succeed to the best of your abilities! It is important to know that a school cannot deny your admission because of your condition if you meet the basic requirements for admission, including application deadlines, grade point averages, and college entrance exam scores. In fact, you don't even need to tell a school you have a disability on your application, unless you want an academic adjustment.

What you must do is keep your grades up and become involved in extracurricular activities—just like any other student. Disabled or not, students must meet school standards for admission.

INTERNATIONAL COLLEGE COUNSELORS NOTE: The Americans with Disabilities Act (ADA) requires educational institutions at all levels, public and private, to provide equal access to their programs, services, and facilities to students, employees, and members of the public, regardless of disability.

TO TELL OR NOT TO TELL

Whether you should reveal your disability early in the admissions process is up to you. The best filter may be: "Will it hurt my chances?" or "Is it helpful to know?"

Disclosure early in the admissions process is often recommended for applicants who need to provide context. For example, a disabled student may need to explain why a standardized test score appears low when compared with outstanding grades.

However, applicants with strong grades and test scores should think twice before disclosing any learning issues, especially if there were no academic repercussions or if they are no longer relevant.

While it is unethical for a school to discriminate based on disability, this does not mean it can't happen. Whichever your decision, consider that you may prefer to attend a school that is going to be sensitive to your disability and help you be successful.

THE APPLICATION

If you decide to disclose it, we recommend that you describe your disability in a letter to the appropriate school personnel and keep a copy of the letter.

You can also call attention to your disability in your main essay. However, if you choose to do this, the essay must be positive and show how you can still succeed. A good answer would be how you were diagnosed with dyslexia in 4th grade and are now in AP English. You may be getting a "C," but the context puts the accomplishment in perspective.

We discuss this more in Chapter 4, but do not try to write an essay designed to make an admissions officer feel sorry for you. This doesn't work.

Also, be prepared to send copies of your psycho-educational evaluation, testing records, and any other assessments of your disabilities directly to the school.

TESTING ADJUSTMENTS FOR STUDENTS WITH DISABILITIES

Students with physical or mental disabilities can receive special accommodations on standardized tests including the following:

▸ SAT

- SAT Subject Tests
- ACT
- PSAT/NMSQT
- Advanced Placement Program (AP) Exams
- ASSET
- COMPASS

ACT/SAT/PSAT/NMSQT/AP Exams

As a student with a disability, you can request accommodations when you schedule your exams. You will be asked to provide documentation of your disability. For details, visit the ACT website (http://www.act.org) and the College Board website (http://www.collegeboard.com).

ASSET and COMPASS

Test-taking accommodations also apply to the ASSET (Assessment of Skills for Successful Entry and Transfer) and COMPASS (Computer Adaptive Placement Assessment and Support System) tests. These are short placement exams often required by community colleges. These exams are designed to help identify your strengths and needs. More information on these exams can be found at:

http://www.act.org/compass
http://www.act.org/asset/index.html.

Testing accommodations may include:

- Individual administration of the test
- Audiocassette tape or large- print test editions
- Special answer sheets
- Extended testing time and breaks
- An interpreter
- Braille editions

INTERNATIONAL COLLEGE COUNSELORS TIP: Whether you were given extra time on the SAT and ACT is information kept confidential by the testing companies. We recommend that you apply for accommodations in 9th or 10th grade. It takes time to apply, gives you time to appeal, and you don't want to take the test without the accommodation for fear you will do <u>too well</u> and not get the accommodation.

Without a doubt, do not take the SAT or ACT if you believe you are eligible for accommodations before getting those accommodations. You see, if you do "well," the SAT and ACT companies will use that as "proof" that you don't need the accommodation. Of course, your version of "well" might be different from that of the College Board.

We once worked with a student named Byron who had straight A's and also a learning disability. He was shooting to attend Harvard or some other Ivy League school. Because Byron was not working with us at the time, he decided to take the SAT before applying for extra time. While Byron did "well" for the College Board, he certainly did not reach the levels he could have with the extra time. Unfortunately, Byron was unable to get his extra time for a subsequent test. Thankfully, since the College Board and ACT are two separate companies, he was able to get the extra time for the ACT and did far better on that exam.

FINANCIAL AID

Don't fear the added costs that may come along with the accommodations you need. Disability-related expenses may be factored in to get increased financial aid. When you apply for financial aid, inform the financial aid administrator of your disability-related expenses. Remember that financial aid will not cover expenses already covered by assisting agencies.

Possible disability-related expenses include:

- Services for personal care attendants
- Special education equipment related to your disability and its

maintenance

▸ Special transportation

▸ Medical expenses relating directly to your disability not covered by insurance

If the financial aid process becomes overwhelming, ask for help. College financial aid staff will answer your questions and help you complete this process. Some states also have private foundations that are set up to help students at no cost.

ONCE YOU'RE ACCEPTED TO COLLEGE

Don't overlook the details. You will need to take certain steps to ensure everything runs smoothly. Students receive services related to a disability only if they:

▸ Contact the coordinator of disability services

▸ Provide the required documentation. (Make sure your tests are updated.)

▸ Request services each term or semester

Unlike public schools, colleges are under no obligation to identify you as a person with a disability. You need to find the college's disability services center and go through their eligibility process before accommodations will be provided. Call the school's office that provides services to students with disabilities for information and help. Keep in mind, reasonable accommodations are intended to "level the playing field" between disabled and non-disabled students. This means the accommodations are designed to help a student with disabilities participate and access a program. It does not mean the essence of a program will be altered with changes in course content or course standards.

Common accommodations include extended time for test-taking, assistive technology, oral reports instead of written reports, and alternate forms of class projects. In college, determining what is reasonable is mostly at the discretion of your professors and disability resource professionals, and they may or may not use available diagnostic information, previous IEPs, and your student input.

Colleges may not charge students with disabilities more for participating in its programs or activities than it charges students who do not have disabilities.

Limitations to Consider

Colleges are not required to do any of the following:

▸ Make any accommodations that would lower or change their academic standards to accommodate a disability.

▸ Make any changes in programs or activities that would fundamentally change the nature of the program.

▸ Provide accommodations that would cause an undue financial burden. This includes personal attendants, readers for personal use or study, or other personal services such as tutoring and typing services.

Chapter 15:
Community College, Alternative Schools, the Gap Year and Alternative Opportunities

You don't have to go to a four-year college right away, and it's never too late. There is no such thing as the perfect time to start college. Some students benefit from a year off to work, study, or travel, and these experiences allow them to be better, more engaged students. Some students choose to apply to college and gain admission and then defer their entrance, while others wait to apply until after they have had an alternative experience.

You don't have to get a four-year college degree to find a career that fits your personality, interests, and talents. You don't need a four-year college degree to have a successful career. While you may want to eventually consider getting a four-year college degree, choosing an alternative course of action is something well worth considering. For some people, the flexibility of these alternatives allows them to explore previously impermeable avenues of career development. Whatever you choose to do, the important thing is that you choose something that keeps your life and career moving in a forward direction.

COMMUNITY COLLEGE

Two-year colleges, also known as junior colleges, are one of the largest and fastest-growing sectors of higher education. Attendance at one can serve as a path to a four-year school or to a career. Starting at a community college also offers a number of other advantages including the following:

Easier admissions requirements
All students are accepted to community college, regardless of past academic performance, if they've graduated high school or have a GED. The SAT and ACT are not required for entrance into many community colleges.

Cost Savings
Tuition and college fees are typically much lower than four-year colleges, even the public ones. Financial assistance, including Pell Grants and scholarships, are also usually available. Community colleges also offer students the opportunity to live at home while attending college, another significant cost-saver.

Opportunity to Explore
Community college offers students a chance to explore their interests before committing to a major. This can save you a lot of money if you are undecided.

Certificates and/or Diplomas
The two-year programs can earn you an associate or liberal arts degree. Curriculum can also include specialized career training and certification. Some schools offer four-year degrees.

Career Guidance
Many community colleges offer extensive support to ensure a student's success, including career guidance, assessments, and a career roadmap.

Transfer Credits
Four-year schools accept community college students as transfer students. Most also accept some or all credits earned at a community college, though each school has different policies regarding the acceptance of credits. See Chapter 17 on Transferring. Some four- year colleges partner with two-year colleges to smooth the transfer process, allowing students to enter as college juniors.

Basic requirement completion
You're going to have to get your general graduation requirements out of the way one way or another. Community colleges are good places to earn these credits.

Transcript Improvement
Taking classes at a community college can help you increase your GPA, so if you didn't meet the minimum admissions requirements at four-

year colleges with your high school grades, you have a second chance. Attending a community college also shows you are serious about your education.

Scholarships and Grants

Good grades in a community college can also help you earn scholarships and grants, a number of which are specified for students who attended community college.

ALTERNATIVE SCHOOLS—SERVICE ACADEMIES

Service academies offer quality education and career training for free. You will also receive free room and board, food, clothing, full medical and dental benefits, and get paid.

But don't ignore the fact that going to a service academy is a huge, life-changing commitment. Your college experience will also be very different in comparison to non-service academies. They are extremely tough—mentally, physically, and emotionally. Furthermore, upon graduation, you are required to serve the U.S.

All service academies have rigorous application processes, and most, but not all, require a nomination from a U.S. Senator, a Congressman, the Vice President, or the President of the United States for acceptance. To get in, you really, really need to demonstrate you want to go and that service is your lifelong dream, though attending one of these schools does not mean you are committed to the military forever.

Service academies include:

- United States Naval Academy (Annapolis)
- United States Air Force Academy
- United States Coast Guard Academy
- United States Merchant Marine Academy
- United States Military Academy at West Point

ALTERNATIVE SCHOOLS—VISUAL OR PERFORMING ARTS SCHOOLS

When it comes to applying to colleges as a prospective visual or performing arts major, you must approach admissions with an abundance of passion for your career. Admission requirements include auditions or portfolios, which can be time-consuming and nerve-wracking.

Most importantly, students need to find the right school for their talents.

Look beyond the elite schools.
Schools such as New York University, Julliard, the Rhode Island School of Design, University of Southern California, University of Michigan, Berklee College of Music, and Carnegie Mellon are the elitist of the elite for certain visual or performing arts. They are the Harvards and Princetons for the arts. In other words, many students want to attend but only a few will be accepted. In any given major—from musical theatre to music—there are other good schools out there. *U.S. News & World Report* offers a listing of specialty schools. Look into the schools on the list called "Unranked Specialty Schools: Arts."

Get an honest opinion on your talents.
Before spending the time and money on applying to college for a visual or performing arts, get an expert or two to critique your talent. It may be better for your future to pursue your passion as a minor or a club activity.

Know what you need for the audition or portfolio.
Know what the school requires for the admissions process. Cooper Union sends you a home test to take when you apply. When you attend an audition, make sure you wear appropriate clothes and perform appropriate material.

124

Attend joint auditions.

Attending a joint audition can help you and your family save money. Joint auditions mean a number of schools that offer a bachelor's degree program in a particular major, get together and hold auditions or review artwork and offer feedback for attendees. Theater majors look i n t o the National Unified Auditions. Visual art and design majors look into National Portfolio Day.

Pay attention to financial aid.

Many art schools and conservatories are expensive. They also tend to offer less financial aid than traditional colleges that offer a wider range of majors. You can successfully develop your passion at traditional schools, so don't ignore them.

GAP YEAR

It's not unusual for students to take some time off before committing to a two- or four-year college. This break is often called a "gap year." The term "gap year" does not always have to mean a full year. Some students take off a semester or whatever period of time they may have to work with. Reasons for taking a gap year typically include: avoiding burnout, finding a passion, satisfying curiosity, and attending to a health or family matter.

INTERNATIONAL COLLEGE COUNSELORS TIP: Even if you plan to take a year off, apply to colleges during your senior year. Getting application materials together and meeting deadlines during high school is much easier then waiting to do this during your gap year. If you are accepted to a school and decide to defer admission, look on the school's website for its policies and requirements. Some schools require your reasons for deferment to be submitted in writing to the dean of admission, along with a deposit. Make sure you meet deadlines to reserve your place in the following year's freshman class. Make sure you understand the school's policies. Not all of them will allow deferred admissions, and some won't give college credit for any work completed during the deferral.

Note, many schools won't allow deferrals for less than a year. If the school does allow you to start midyear, on-campus housing or financial aid may not be available. Check with the financial aid office and find out what impact, if any, taking a year off will have. If you have been offered financial assistance, it may not be guaranteed the next year. Applications may need to be updated, and any money you earn during your year off may affect financial aid eligibility.

Gap year options range from different activities to different lengths of time. Some of the more common gap year options include:

Secure an internship.
An internship is a paid or unpaid position that gives you the opportunity to explore your interests and/or get some training for your future career. If you're thinking about getting an internship before you go to college, look for employers where you can explore a specific interest. See Chapter 10 for more information on internships.

Travel.
Visiting new places, in the U.S. and abroad, is a great way to gain valuable life experience and gain perspective on what you want to do. There are many ways to explore the world, some of which don't require a lot of money. Options include student exchange programs, teaching English abroad, volunteering with an international group, becoming a nanny for a family in another country, or taking a job on a cruise ship. If you do travel, make sure you get to know the local customs and culture. Learning a foreign language can give you a huge boost up the career ladder.

Important note: If you do look for exchange or employment opportunities abroad, make sure you work with a reputable company.

Volunteer.
You can gain valuable experience and explore possible career paths through volunteer work. There are many opportunities to make a difference. National programs like AmeriCorps, American Red Cross, the Salvation Army, and the Student Conservation Association (SCA)

offer the chance for service. There are also many local opportunities. If you're thinking about volunteering, consider options that allow you to explore a specific interest, such as health care, teaching, or environmental conservation. A number of websites can help you find volunteer opportunities. Type "volunteer work find" into a search engine and see what results come up.

Attend a gap year program.

A number of companies have gap year programs designed to help students find gap year opportunities. A year planned by one of these companies can include work opportunities, study abroad, cultural study programs, language classes, and more. Gap year programs typically cost less than a year of college, but they can still be pricey. To find some of these programs, type "gap year programs" into a search engine.

Start your own business.

Beat your own career path by starting your own business. There are many entrepreneurial business opportunities. What you need to do is find your own niche. If you decide to go this route, you must do your research and work out a potential business plan. Consider your strengths, interests, and skills honestly.

ALTERNATIVE EDUCATION OPPORTUNITIES

Apprenticeship

Apprenticeships mean learning on the job, and they aren't just for blacksmiths. If you have an interest in a particular trade, such as computers or construction, you have the option to take an apprenticeship or seek out jobs in the trade. Apprenticeships will give you valuable experience through in-depth training and guide you toward advancement by helping you with the certifications or licenses you need to succeed.

Some professions for which apprenticeships are typical:

- Construction

- Pharmacy assistant (many go on to study to become full-fledged

127

pharmacists)

- Plumber
- Carpenter
- Photographer
- Animal breeder
- Baker
- Barber
- Jeweler
- Mechanic

Trade School
Specialized trade schools offer classes and specialized training to enter certain careers. Programs include automobile repair, computers, technology, and cosmetology.

Certification and Massive Online Open Courses (MOOCs)
If you are considering professions like life coaching or personal training, look online to see what options you have for certification. You can also take online courses. This is a good way to explore your interests and continue your education at the same time. There are a number of opportunities to take courses for free. Look into Massive Open Online Courses, also called MOOCs. Schools including MIT, Harvard, Duke, Yale, Stanford, UCLA, John Hopkins, and the University of Virginia offer these classes, many of which are free via the Internet, in subjects ranging from artificial intelligence and chemistry to finance and sociology. A few of the larger organizations offering MOOCs are Coursera, edX, and Udacity.

Job
If you're thinking about getting a job before you go to college, move away from the companies that usually hire teens for part-time work to employers where you can either start on a career or explore a specific interest. At this stage, no job is too small. Even those who start in the

mailroom can work their way up. (For want-to-be talent agents in Hollywood, starting in the talent agency mailroom is sometimes a requirement.) Start with employers whose services or products interest you.

Military

By joining the military, you can serve your country, learn new skills, accrue valuable work experience, forge a career path, and/or earn money toward a future college education. But don't ignore that joining the military is a huge, life-changing commitment. Make sure you understand what you're committing to before you sign anything.

Chapter 16:
Choosing a Major

There are a number of students who say they "always knew" what they wanted to do with their lives. As such, it's easy for them to know what they want to major in. Then there are the majority of students—those with no idea what they really want to do with their lives.

Either way, it's not the end of the world.

What's best is that you pick a major for the college application.

Schools prefer that you fill in a college major because they like to see that you have career ambitions. This is especially important if you are applying to a competitive school or program. I always advise students to pick a major on their applications.

Don't panic if you don't have a major. Understand the game. Picking a major for your college application doesn't mean you're committed to it forever. You are not locked into anything you write on the college admissions form. Most college students change their major at least once in their college careers. Many others change their major several times. Schools also have double majors, and some have triple majors. You can minor in a subject, as well.

Keep your eye on the prize. The college admissions goal is to get into the school of your dreams. Once you're in, you'll have flexibility.

Choosing a major and exploring careers are main reasons you go to college in the first place!

INTERNATIONAL COLLEGE COUNSELORS TIP: Once you get into a school, changing majors may mean giving up a scholarship, so you need to weigh your options and consider the timing when it comes to switching majors. The most important thing is that the school you attend has the major you ultimately choose. You don't want to find, senior year, that you love architecture but your school does not have an architecture program. Thinking ahead can save you time and money on transfer applications!

While we understand that students might be unable to know exactly what they want to do when they graduate, we do like them to have a general idea. The reason is that you don't want to attend a college that does not have a major of interest. For example, if you want to do engineering, it would be great if the college offers engineering. Otherwise, you have to transfer or attend graduate school.

We once worked with a student named Shira who was unsure of what she wanted to major in. She could not decide, and when pressed, simply shut down. What we recommended is that Shira attend a large college with lots of majors and course offerings. In this way, she could try a bunch of new courses and not be limited by what the school had to offer.

CHOOSING A MAJOR: WHAT YOU NEED TO DO

To make the college journey easier for yourself, you need to narrow down your choices. Your goal is to make a list of a few majors that interest you the most. Then you want to explore those few majors in greater depth before making any commitments.

Examine your interests.

▸ What are your interests? What are your passions? What types of things excite you? What activities do you make time for and seek out on your own? What do you feel comfortable with?

▸ Think about your classes. Was there one you liked best? Was it math, science, French, or literature?

▸ Think about your hobbies. Do you love programming apps, collecting insects, or designing business cards? Do you like hiking outdoors, meeting new people, or decorating?

▸ What do you like to read about? Do you like astronomy or nature? Fashion or technology?

> What extracurricular activities and clubs were especially enjoyable to you?

Examine your abilities.

> Be 100-percent honest. What are you good at? What are your strengths? What are your weaknesses? What unique skills or abilities do you have? Are there things that you're better at than most people?

> When thinking about your abilities, think about all parts of your life—from the extracurricular activities you participated in to the things you learned about yourself from summer jobs.

> What school courses were you best in? Are you a natural leader? Do you have an above-average ability to stay organized? Are you good with animals, numbers, or seeing patterns in behavior?

> Everyone has different preferences and skills. Choosing a major that requires those abilities will put you at an advantage. A superhero gifted with flying abilities doesn't say, "I think I'll be the spider guy."

Examine what you value in life and work.

Examples of values include: being around people, attention to detail, helping others, working under pressure, being creative, stability, security, status, being part of a group, and many others. You'll most prefer a career that aligns with your values.

Explore the careers that interest you.

Imagine doing something you love and getting paid to do it. What would that something be? What kind of work appeals to you?

Did you see something on TV and think that looks like something you could see yourself doing? Does a family friend have a job you'd like? Are you planning to take over a family business?

If you are passionate about a particular field, consider all aspects of the career path. Healthcare, for example, is more than medicine. You could become a researcher, a pharmaceutical representative, or a hospital HR manager. A sports career job title isn't only "athlete." You could become a sports trainer, nutritionist, sports journalist, or event planner. Directing and acting aren't the only film-industry careers. Stay after a film and really watch the credits. You'll see a lot of different jobs and titles on there.

Do your research.

- Talk to students. Locate college students who are studying in the majors you are interested in.

- Review a college's course catalog. This will give you an idea of all the majors to choose from. It will also give you insight on what the required courses are and the specialized tracks.

- Talk to your academic adviser.

- Consult with family and friends. They know you best and can offer good insight into who you are and what you are good at.

- Go online. On the Internet there is a vast amount of resources on majors and careers.

- Connect. Be proactive. See if you can get in touch with someone who has the career or job you're interested in. Send them a nice note, and maybe you'll get a reply.

- Attend meetings of academically focused clubs, such as Future Doctors or Future Business Leaders.

- Attend career-related events like speaking tours or seminars. Oftentimes you can find these listed on community event calendars.

- Get tested. There are many self-assessment tests, free and paid, that can help you determine what you might want to do for your career.

- The Riley Guide http://www.rileyguide.com/assess.html is one such test with links to various other test-assessment websites.

► Attend a career fair.

► See if you can spend time after school or during winter/
spring/summer break shadowing someone who has a career that
interests you.

Do a reality check.
Be realistic and honest. If you don't like kids, cross "elementary school
teacher" off your list. If you're not a competitive person, you aren't
going to thrive in investment banking, dance, or public relations. If you
don't like science or math, then no matter how promising and lucrative
STEM studies sound, you're going to be miserable. The same goes for
being a doctor; you need to be good at science to study medicine. If
you're not into detail-oriented work, avoid event planning. If you're not
organized in your personal life, it's going to be hard to do human
resources. Sometimes there are ways to overcome the obstacles, but it
is important to really consider and evaluate if you can—and want—to
do so.

Start by looking at all the courses you'll need in order to graduate with
a certain major.

Consider the future.
While everyone wants to do what they love, do not disregard the
importance of money or how hard it is to "make it" in certain careers.
You may love musical theatre, but there are very few people who can
make it a full-time career.

If you have your heart set on something, it doesn't necessarily mean you
shouldn't try. But you must move forward knowing the realistic
outcome. The same goes for choosing a very, very specific career—
studying wild dolphins, for example. It doesn't mean you won't find a
job, but it will most likely be hard to find the perfect job match. If you
go this route, be prepared to compromise.

Someone who studies oceanography may consider teaching it one day.

Someone who studies drama may find their outlet in community theatre while they support themselves in an unrelated field.

A handy, helpful, and free reality-check guide.
A good online resource for careers is Bureau of Labor Statistics' Occupational Outlook Handbook. It includes data on hundreds of jobs, including the training and education needed, salary, what workers do on the job, working conditions, and expected job prospects. Go to http://www.bls.gov/oco.

Narrow your choices and choose a major.
Once you've gone through all the above steps, you should have a better idea of the major you are interested in pursuing.

And, as I said before, if you're really torn, consider a double major, satisfy an interest with a minor, or look forward to grad school.

INTERNATIONAL COLLEGE COUNSELORS TIP: Even if choosing a major for your application is not a lifetime commitment, this does not mean you shouldn't choose your major carefully. For students majoring in high-demand fields like technology, medicine, education, and science, there may be money available from private loan-forgiveness programs, state and federal grants, specific scholarships and other sources. For example, the federal government provides funds to future educators through the Teacher Education Assistance for College and Higher Education (TEACH) Grant Program. Individual states offer similar college-financing initiatives for future nurses, public defenders, healthcare workers, and other careers. Professional organizations and nonprofits also offer awards to students in specific fields of study.

Chapter 17:
Transferring

This is a good chapter for students who want to transfer or are planning to transfer. For all students: It's good to know you have choices. Even after getting into a college, accepting the offer, and attending, you can change your mind if a school is not the right fit for you.

Why do students transfer?
Some main reasons why students choose to transfer schools:

▸ The current school does not have a strong program in an area of interest.

▸ Academics are too challenging or not challenging enough.

▸ The school is too expensive.

▸ Students were rejected from becoming freshmen at their first-choice school and choose to attend another school with the intention of transferring.

▸ Students go from a two-year college to a four-year one.

▸ Students want to enroll in a college with a bigger name or higher ranking.

▸ Students are socially unhappy—for example, if a rural campus proves too isolating.

▸ Students want or need to be closer to home.

MAKING THE DECISION

Make sure you're transferring for the right reasons. If transferring wasn't part of your original college plan, start by thinking through all aspects of the move. Assess your reasons, and make sure they're compelling enough to make the inconveniences and cost of transferring worthwhile.

PLANNING YOUR COLLEGE TRANSFER

Keep track of the deadlines.
Deadlines vary from school to school. For most schools, begin the application process in October if you want to attend classes during the winter semester. To begin in the fall semester, start the process in January. You will most likely need to send in an application by March or April if you plan to transfer in the fall.

Understand the financial aid options for transfer students. (More on this below in Financial Considerations.)

Check the credit policy.
Colleges have different policies for transfer students. Usually they expect you to have acquired a minimum of credits. Know what your prospective schools expect, and understand what you'll need regarding courses, credits, and GPA. (More on this later.)

Get the grades.
Transferring to another college is not like applying to college the first time. Your college transcript will be given more weight than your high school transcript and test scores. Be prepared to provide transcripts of all of the schools you have attended, including high school.

Measure up the numbers.
Prepare to measure up to the numbers if you want to transfer to a higher- ranked school. If your high school grades were not high enough, you will need to make high grades in college.

Get involved.
Get involved at your current school as if it were your dream school. Colleges look more favorably on students with leadership roles and activities. You don't want to be seen as a sourpuss who was moping in a dorm room for the past year.

Make connections.
You will likely need recommendations from one or two professors. Make connections with professors at your current school.

Explore options.
Approach transferring with your eyes wide open; not all schools are easy to transfer into.

Timing.
Consider waiting until your junior year to attempt a transfer to a highly competitive school. Most colleges provide more open spaces for transfers in that year. Also, you probably won't have to submit your high school grades and test scores.

Visit schools.
Once you have decided to transfer and have a list of new schools, visit each campus and be sure to sit in on the specific classes that interest you.

You don't want to find yourself transferring again.

COURSE/CREDIT TRANSFER

One of the biggest considerations in a college transfer is credit. Don't assume all your credits will transfer. Not all classes or credits are transferable, and some schools won't accept credit from a class if you earned less than a C. Some schools only accept credits for classes similar to those they offer. The more specialized the class, the less chance a school will accept the credits.

Know, too, that many colleges set a limit to the number of transfer credit hours they'll allow. You'll want to know if you're over the limit. I recommend you meet with an academic counselor or advisor at the college you want to transfer to in order to determine which of your credits may transfer. Call the school and ask what their policy is regarding this before accepting an admissions offer.

Your best bet is to send your transcript to the appropriate department faculty members or admissions advisors and request a credit evaluation in writing. Doing this credit assessment before you start your new school can prevent you from taking repeat or overlapping courses and potentially save you tuition money.

For some courses you may receive elective credit only. This means you may find yourself with enough credits to graduate, without having fulfilled your new school's general education or major requirements. Make sure you ask specifically how many additional credits you will be required to complete to earn your degree.

As a general rule, grade point average does not transfer. If you transfer, you will most likely start at your new school with a 0.0 GPA. Information on credit transfer can usually be found on a college's website.

If you have one dream school in mind:
If you are planning a transfer before you begin taking classes and you have one goal school in mind, ask the appropriate authority at your choice school to preapprove courses for credit transfer. See if you can work with that person to set up a course load. However, keep the door open for the possibility that you'll want or need to finish at your current school; it is best to try and take courses that work at both schools.

TRANSFERRING FROM A COMMUNITY COLLEGE TO A FOUR-YEAR UNIVERSITY

Some states have articulation agreements between four-year universities and community colleges, and students can check online to see courses that automatically transfer.

More specifically, some community colleges have a dual admissions agreement with four-year institutions, where qualified students can be simultaneously accepted to both schools and become automatically enrolled in the four-year school after they complete their associate

139

degree.

Research whether your community college has an articulation agreement or a collaborative agreement with the university you'd like to attend. Articulation agreements outline specific courses a university will accept from a two-year institution and guarantee admission once the two-year curriculum has been completed. Collaborative agreements may not guarantee admission but will designate courses the school will accept as transfer of credit.

ACING THE TRANSFER ADMISSIONS PROCESS

Avoid common (and often-made) mistakes.

- Don't miss any deadlines.
- Make sure you send your transcripts to the right office.

Get the right letters of recommendation.
For your transfer application, get recommendations from your college professors. These carry more weight than high school recommendations. Approach professors with whom you have a good rapport, especially ones in your academic discipline. If a professor agrees to write a recommendation for you, make sure you thank him or her, verbally before the letter is written and in writing, after.

Write the transfer essay.
A transfer essay should present a clear and specific reason for wanting to transfer. Good reasons for transferring usually include academic and non-academic opportunities you believe the new college offers. Do not write about love of sports teams, wanting to be near a girl or boyfriend, or why you dislike your current school. You can say your current school isn't a good match for your interests and goals, but be extra- careful not to sound critical, harsh, or bitter.

If you had any problems at your current school, take responsibility for them. As necessary, explain how you plan to improve your performance at your new school.

Schools like to see that you've matured as a person and as a student. Good topics to hit on include your leadership qualities, your involvement at your school, and your sincere efforts to fit in and make the best of the opportunity you had. Any time attending college should be considered an opportunity.

Your writing also needs to show that you know the school to which you are applying. Make sure you research the school well and put details in your essay. If you can replace the name of one college with another, you haven't written a good transfer essay.

Make sure your essay is error-free before you send it.

ENTERING A DREAM SCHOOL THROUGH THE BACK DOOR

This approach does not have a 100-percent guarantee, but if you desperately want to attend a school and have been rejected as a transfer student, it's worth a try.

Take evening courses or continuing education credits at your dream school that match courses offered for credit. The goal is to accrue approximately forty hours of credit toward your intended major, then apply to the school as a degree candidate. Note that this can vary depending on the number of credits you already have.

Before you choose to go this route, I recommend you (1) apply to the school as a transfer student, and (2) discuss this possibility with your dream school. Only if you feel good about what you hear should you attempt this approach.

Chapter 18:
Financial Aid
(or How to Go to College without Going Broke)
Grants, Loans, and More

In this chapter, I am going to give you an overview of financial aid and the opportunities available. Getting into the details would require an extra book, and many are available just on this subject.

In most cases, you can't afford not to go to college. But, taking on too much debt and ending up living in your parent's house after college is not the only option. You could become a Westinghouse scholar, Olympic champion, or dictator of a small country. Then you'd get a free ride. Schools love world-ranked athletes, internationally or nationally recognized students, talented musicians, and others with unique skills, abilities, and backgrounds. Schools also want underrepresented minority students.

Then there are the majority of us.

For the less driven or genetically gifted, there's hope for you too: you need to maximize your financial aid and minimize your costs. Getting out of college with little or no debt is hard, but not impossible.

In fact, don't choose which colleges to apply to based on the cost of tuition alone. Schools base financial aid on the difference between the cost and what a family is expected to pay. Before making any decisions, you need to separate the advertised price of tuition and the net cost, which factors in grants and scholarships. Don't make any decisions until after you receive your financial aid award letters and compare them.

While private schools appear to be more expensive than public schools, most have significant amounts of need-based and merit-based aid. You may just find the private school to be less expensive than the public schools that can't provide the aid. Some private schools discount their tuition as much as 50 percent, which reflects their way of competing with other schools. No school wants to lose quality students, if the college can afford it.

Be open to all the possibilities each college offers.

Be realistic too. Discounts are typically based on a combo of academic merit and financial need. Students with strong high school grades and standardized test scores and high financial need most often receive the best financial aid support.

INTERNATIONAL COLLEGE COUNSELORS NOTE: Look for three categories of assistance in the award letter: gift aid (grants and/or scholarships), work-study job opportunities, and loans. But remember, financial aid offers are for freshman year only, and contain no promises about what financial aid will look like in future years.

ESTIMATING THE COSTS

Before you send in an acceptance letter, you and your family need to know the bottom line. What is the real cost to attend a school?

All colleges are required by law to post a "net price calculator" on their websites. The net price is an estimate based on the cost of attendance and financial aid policies for the award year. Using the calculator, you should be able to get an idea of the cost of attendance and your eligibility for financial assistance. Once you calculate the real costs, you may find that the college that seems prohibitively expensive is actually more affordable than you thought.

Keep in mind, not all calculators are created equally. The results from the calculators are only estimates, and colleges can calculate them differently, so use them to make rough comparisons between colleges.

THE STUDENT DEBT CALCULATOR

In addition to using a net price calculator, make sure you take advantage of the free online financial aid calculator from the Consumer Financial

Protection Bureau. It was created as part of the "Know Before You Owe" initiative. See:

http://www.consumerfinance.gov/payingforcollege.

This online financial aid calculator will give you a larger picture of how costs vary at the colleges you're considering, and how much debt you're likely to have after you graduate.

Programmed into the calculator is information on over 7,500 schools. You can enter up to three colleges at a time for comparison. The tool will automatically compare those choices with the national average for schools of their types.

The calculator will show you what your estimated monthly loan payment could end up being, based on the cost of tuition, room and board, books, supplies, other expenses, and the average amount of grants and scholarships awarded at that particular college.

To make the results more accurate and personalized, you will want to enter your own financial aid information.

To understand the shortcomings of the calculator, make sure you read the detailed explanation of the tool's functions.

ESTIMATING A COLLEGE'S VALUE

The College Scorecard is a planning web tool from the U.S. Department of Education. It is designed to provide more information about a college's affordability in regards to value.

The Scorecard offers information on five key pieces of data about a college: costs, graduation rate, loan default, average amount borrowed, and employment. These are important elements to consider when choosing a college.

Students and their families start by entering the name of a college of interest or selecting factors that are important in their college search.

HOW TO MAKE COLLEGE MORE AFFORDABLE

The top ways to make college more affordable include:

- ► Government loans

- ► Grants

- ► College aid in the form of loans, grants or work study

- ► Scholarships

In this chapter, I will discuss all the above EXCEPT for scholarships. You'll find everything you need to know about scholarships in Chapter 19.

AN OVERVIEW OF LOANS

While grants and scholarships are always desirable, as you don't need to pay them back, the best loan option is different for each family. Loans need to be repaid with interest. Which loan option is best is determined by your family's unique situation.

It's healthy to have concerns about borrowing money and taking on loan debt. It's also worth recognizing that it's a viable option to help you achieve your academic goals. It is possible to borrow responsibly and minimize the total amount you'll have to repay.

INTERNATIONAL COLLEGE COUNSELORS NOTE: If a school says they meet 100 percent of financial need, and it includes loans, they don't mean you will pay nothing. You will need to pay back any loans, with interest.

Let's begin with getting to know the different types of loans.

There are two main categories of loans: need-based and non-need-based.

Need-based loans are for those students whose families have financial need. These typically have better terms, so consider them first. The lower the interest rate, the less expensive the loan and the less you have to repay.

Non-need-based loans are to help families pay if they can't afford to pay college costs from current income and savings.

There are three main types of college loans: government loans, college loans, and private loans. Try the government loans first!

INTERNATIONAL COLLEGE COUNSELORS NOTE: Don't take more loans than you have to. Loans should only be used for unavoidable expenses such as tuition and fees, room and board, and perhaps sometimes books. A career-building summer internship or a fellowship may also qualify as a good loan reason. Consider your starting salary in your chosen field before borrowing any money. Also consider whether you will need to attend grad school or not. You don't want to spend all your money on your undergrad schooling.

GOVERNMENT LOANS

Federal loans are the cheapest student loans with rates that are usually fixed. Federal student loans also can be capped at 15 percent of a student's "discretionary income." That's defined as earnings above 150 percent of the poverty line.

Federal subsidized Stafford Loans are need-based loans. The government pays the yearly interest while you're in school.

Federal unsubsidized Stafford Loans are sponsored by the government but are not based on financial need. Unsubsidized Stafford Loans can be used to help pay your family's share of costs. You're responsible for paying interest on the loan while in school, unless you choose to have the interest added to the principal during your years at school. If you do this, you are borrowing the amount of the interest as well, and that means you end up repaying more money. Both subsidized and

146

unsubsidized Stafford Loans can be used to pay for tuition and fees, room and board, books and supplies, transportation, and living allowance.

Federal Perkins Loans are awarded by colleges to students with the highest need, using limited pools of money. The interest rate is very low, and you don't make any loan payments while in school.

Parent PLUS Loans allow families to borrow up to the total cost of education minus any financial aid received. These government-sponsored loans are not based on need.

Federal PLUS Loans are the largest source of parent loans. The interest rate is fixed, meaning it's attractive when compared to many of the other borrowing options.

How to Get A Government Loan

The U.S. government loans money to every student who needs it. Two of the most important and most common ways of getting access to government money are the FAFSA and the CSS/Profile.

To receive FAFSA aid (Free Application for Federal Student Aid), you need to fill out a form and file online at http://www.fafsa.gov. This federal application for financial aid is also used to apply for aid from other sources, such as your state or school.

The CSS/Financial Aid Profile, CSS/Profile, or College Scholarship Service Profile is also an application that allows students to apply for financial aid. It is distributed by the College Board and is much more detailed than the FAFSA.

Most private schools require both the FAFSA and the CSS/Profile in order to be eligible to receive financial aid.

The FAFSA determines Federal funding and the Expected Family Contribution (EFC) and is set by the government. The FAFSA does not take into account home equity, medical expenses, or change in employment.

The CSS/Profile helps determine institutional money, in many cases. The EFC calculation may vary by institution, and can take into account home equity, deductions for medical expenses, and provisions for special circumstances.

Just to get the best picture of what the actual cost of attendance will be at a private college, you will need to complete the application process, file your FAFSA, and complete the financial-aid process at the schools you are interested in attending.

With both of these forms, it is important to fill them out as early as possible.

The CSS/Profile has varying deadlines depending on the school and becomes available in the fall. If you are applying early admissions or early decision, the CSS/Profile is often due by November 15. The CSS/Profile can be found at the College Board website: https://profileonline.collegeboard.com/prf/index.jsp.

The FAFSA always becomes available January 1 and should be submitted as soon as data is ready.

If you have specific questions, much like with the CSS/Profile, the folks at FAFSA are EXTREMELY helpful. Please do not hesitate to call the contact numbers or email for help.
FAFSA help: http://www.fafsa.ed.gov/help.htm
CSS/Profile help: http://www.collegeboard.org/contact-us/#css

A family should fill out BOTH of these forms each year if you desire aid for college. Be sure to check your specific school's website for further forms or information. Some schools do require additional forms.

FAFSA OVERVIEW

The FAFSA is one long application with many very detailed questions that require detailed information. But, don't be discouraged. Thousands and thousands and thousands of students before you have successfully filled it out and received government money. So it's not impossible, and if you start early, you will have enough time to get it completed without getting overstressed.

Why did the government make it so hard? The FAFSA was designed to be hard to fill out to discourage fraud. In short, the FAFSA is the starting point to a limited pool of government money that was earmarked to help families pay for college. That pool includes scholarships, grants, and subsidized student loans like the Stafford Loan. It is a limited pool of money, and a lot of people want to swim in a share. The government is not trying to discourage you so much that you'll give up.

Don't leave it until the last minute and it'll all be OK.

INTERNATIONAL COLLEGE COUNSELORS TIP: ALL students should fill the FAFSA out regardless of their household income. A number of scholarships, including some merit scholarships, require the FAFSA as well.

The deadline to file the Free Application for Federal Student Aid is February 1. June 30 is the official government deadline, but for many schools—including Boston University, Brandeis, and Carnegie Mellon—it is February 1. If you do not get your form in by this date, you may not be eligible to receive certain merit scholarships or school financial aid. The FAFSA form is necessary to apply for Pell Grants, Stafford Loans, Perkins Loans, work-study programs, and much state aid.

To find out which Merit Scholarships are tied to filling out the FAFSA, check the college websites.

I repeat: ALL students should fill out the FAFSA no matter what their household income is, if they would like to be eligible for aid.

There is no penalty for filling out the FAFSA whether you receive aid or not. Many students are surprised by the aid they are eligible to receive. And then you can choose to use this aid or not.

The FAFSA is free. You do not need to pay for it.

Completing the FAFSA
An introductory publication for students provides free instructions on how to complete the FAFSA. This is found at the FAFSA website.

Filling Out the FAFSA
Before submitting the FAFSA, double-check EVERYTHING.

In addition to gathering financial information, you will need a FAFSA account and PIN. Go to FAFSA.gov to get one.

INTERNATIONAL COLLEGE COUNSELORS TIP: All financial information needs to be for the previous financial year. Students filing for the FAFSA need documentation from the previous tax year. If you don't have your W-2 tax forms as needed, you can estimate by using pay stubs and then file a FAFSA correction later.

While filling out the FAFSA, you will need the following:

- Your Social Security card. Make sure you enter the number correctly!
- Your driver's license (if any)
- The requested W-2 forms and other records of money earned
- Your (and your spouse's, if you are married) 2010 Federal Income Tax Return
- IRS 1040, 1040A, 1040 EZ
- Your Foreign Tax Return, or Tax Return for Puerto, Guam, American Samoa, the U.S. Virgin Islands, the Marshall Islands, the Federal States of Micronesia, or Palua (if applicable)

- Your parents' Federal Income Tax Return (if you are a dependent student)

- Your untaxed income records

- Your current bank statements

- Your current business and investment mortgage information, business and farm records, stock, bond, and other investment records

- Your alien registration or permanent resident card (if you are not a U.S. citizen)

Over 16 million students and families apply for federal financial aid every year. The government estimates that 1.5 million potential college students could be eligible for Pell Grants but have not applied, perhaps because of the complicated paperwork.

INTERNATIONAL COLLEGE COUNSELORS TIP: Apply for financial aid as early as possible. Most schools have a set amount of financial aid they can give out each year, and once it's given out, there's no more until the next year. However, don't apply so fast that you have errors on your forms. If you have to submit your forms a second time with corrections, you'll be that much more behind.

COLLEGE LOANS

Most colleges offer a low-interest loan that you don't need to pay off until you're out of school. If loans are part of your financial aid package, ask the college about the terms of repayment via email so you can have the answers in writing. Also check out other options so you can find the best solution for you.

Report any private scholarships you earn to your college. Most colleges will subtract the scholarship money from the loan part of your financial aid package, doing this until your loan is gone.

PRIVATE LOANS

I recommend private loans as a last resort. While you can find some with favorable terms, most often the interest rates and fees charged are higher than those for federal loans.

Private loans are generally not subsidized or based on need. While often intended for students, a parent is usually a cosigner, since good credit is often a requirement to get a private loan. If you fail to pay back the loan, your parent/co-signer is responsible for repaying it.

If you need a private loan, make sure you do a careful comparison. Make sure you understand the interest rate, fees, interest rate capitalization policy, repayment period, prepayment penalties, and other terms and conditions before you sign anything.

Private education loans are available from banks, schools, and other financial institutions. Again, these loans usually have a higher interest rate than federal loans.

Some have favorable borrowing terms, but make sure you read everything carefully. (I repeat myself because this is so important.) If there is anything you don't understand, find someone who can explain the details to you.

If you take private loans, look for reliable, vetted companies that are approved by the college's financial aid office or have been recommended by a trusted financial advisor.

GRANTS

Grants are better than loans because you don't have to pay the money back. (Free money!) But, there is a catch: they are not available to everyone.

Pell Grants are federal grants awarded strictly on the student's financial need. Other federal grant programs include the Federal Supplemental Educational Opportunity Grant (also based on financials), and grant programs for students with good grades in competitive high-school programs or specific fields of study, such as math, nursing, or teaching. States and colleges also have their own pools of grant money. Like loans, grants are awarded based on the FAFSA results.

States also offer various grant and scholarship programs. These may be based on your residency status, the location of the college you are attending, or your financial need. If your grant or scholarship needs to be applied for each year, make sure you do it.

Federal and state scholarships and grants do not have to be repaid. Scholarships and grants can also be awarded by community organizations, businesses, or the college you have applied to. The award may be based on financial need and/or merit. It is important for you to know if the award is for one year or several years and if you have to reapply for the funds every year. Make sure you know with certainty if your award depends on any factors such as financial need, your major, participation in an activity, or any other mandatory requirements.

If you receive a grant from your college, make sure you ask the financial aid office—by e-mail, so you have it in writing—to explain which grants in the aid offer will automatically renew in subsequent years, and what the requirements are for that to happen.

COLLEGE AID

The most common types of aid offered by colleges are scholarships, grants, loans, tuition waivers, awards, and work-study.

Need-based aid is awarded after a school determines the financial "need" of a student. A financial aid formula is used to calculate the difference between the cost of attending and the amount of money the college believes your family can afford. In this decision, the school will consider state and federal grants, scholarships, and other sources of funding. Then they will adjust their financial aid offerings accordingly.

Different schools use different aid formulas to determine what they think a student can pay.

Merit-based financial aid is awarded by colleges without regard for financial need. Students who receive this type of aid typically have outstanding academic achievements in high school, special talents such as fine arts (music, theatre, dance, etc.), athletic skills, or FIRST competition experience (FIRST Robotics, FIRST Tech, or FIRST Lego).

Most colleges offer interest-free monthly payment plans, meaning you can spread your payments over ten or twelve months, or whatever the college offers. The student accounts office at the college can answer your questions on this.

Work-Study programs provide students with part-time employment at the college to help with college expenses. The job helps you pay off part of your tuition. Working on campus gives you more flexibility than working off campus because your campus employers are usually more understanding of class schedules and campus activities.

There are two kinds of work-study programs: Federal Work-Study (FWS) and non-Federal Work-Study or Campus Employment.

Federal Work-Study is a form of financial aid awarded to students who demonstrate financial need and meet certain eligibility requirements. You must submit the FAFSA to determine your eligibility for Federal Work-Study. (Yet another reason you should fill out the FAFSA). Apply for a Federal Work-Study position as early as you can. At many colleges, Federal Work-Study funds may be limited.

Non-Federal Work-Study/Campus Employment is not based on financial need. If you do not qualify for Federal Work-Study, you should inquire about non-federal student employment opportunities at your school.

Students should keep in mind that school and work can be difficult to manage, and they must learn how to balance them.

INTERNATIONAL COLLEGE COUNSELORS NOTE: You can take, reduce, or turn down any part of a college's financial aid offer!

MERIT AID

If you are a student looking for merit aid, here are tips that can improve your chances of receiving merit aid.

Do research and find the schools that offer merit aid to students. Your best—and most accurate—bet is to search each college's financial aid site. Some publications like The New York Times and U.S. News & World Report create lists and charts of colleges and universities that award merit aid.

Parents, or students themselves, can also call the school's admissions office or financial aid office and get a general answer on whether a student would be eligible for any merit aid.

Search http://www.MeritAid.com. As its name suggests, this is a good resource for merit aid.

Choose colleges where you'd be at the top. If your grades and tests scores put you in the top 25 percent of the student body, there is a very good chance a school will try to woo you with merit aid.

Take stock of your abilities. Merit aid also means athletic achievements and special talents. If you are skilled in sports, music, etc., merit aid and scholarships focusing on these abilities are worth looking into.

Consider your interests. Your sports, hobbies, clubs, etc. may all offer scholarships. Among the countless activities and associations that offer merit aid are beauty pageants, service clubs, religious groups, honor societies, and 4-H.

Leverage your achievements.
Make a list of the activities you've committed yourself to. There may be merit aid that awards your focused effort.

Evaluate merit-aid scholarships that promote diversity.
You may find you qualify for many merit scholarships simply because of who you are or where you live. A number of schools use merit aid to attract students who are different from the majority of their student body. Qualifications may include being from out of state, being a minority, and gender.

See if your major has merit aid.
A number of merit scholarships are earmarked for students with a particular major.

Look into merit aid offered by state governments.
Accessing this money typically requires you to meet certain GPA, test score, and residence requirements. Two examples: (1) Graduating high school students in the state of Florida may receive a Bright Futures scholarship for most public and private colleges in Florida if they earn at least a 3.0 average in high school, and (2) New York State Scholarships for Academic Excellence program provides top scholars with $1,500 scholarships to study at in-state colleges.

Retake the SAT or ACT as necessary.
Higher grades and test scores may generate more aid. A number of schools even state this on their websites.

Apply, apply, apply for scholarships.
These are a form of merit aid under another name. We mentioned a few roads to scholarships previously, but there are literally thousands of scholarships with all sorts of eligibility requirements.

Negotiate.
If you have received admission letters from two or more schools of equivalent standards, don't be afraid to "bargain." Some schools may be willing to match a merit grant offered by another school.

THE FINANCIAL AID "DON'T" LIST

Don't procrastinate when it comes to financial aid.
Senior year is not the time to start thinking about making financial aid decisions. Planning financial aid eligibility should start AT LATEST when the student is in 10th or 11th grade. By getting a head start on understanding financial aid and avoiding the most common financial aid mistakes, you can get the best financial aid package possible based on the tentative choices for college. Given the rising cost of college over the years, the tuition of out-of-state public schools is almost on par with private schools.

Keep in mind: the criteria for how state schools distribute aid are very different from those for private schools.

Don't miss the deadlines.
Make sure you keep track of them, and don't wait for the last minute here either. Technical difficulties and "acts of God" typically fall on deaf ears at the financial aid offices. If you miss the deadlines, you may eliminate yourself from receiving aid.

Don't base the financial aid you may or may not receive on the aid any friends did or did not receive.
Each financial aid eligibility situation is entirely unique.

Don't assume that you are eligible for 100 percent of tuition-covering aid.
Even if you're class valedictorian, captain of the football team, an oboe player, and a state science fair winner, this is unrealistic. If you do want to have at least one affordable college choice that requires little or no financial aid, apply for a state-supported college in your home state.

Don't count on your relatives to pay for your tuition.
Unexpected circumstances come up even for relatives with the best intentions. So even if a relative has agreed to pay for your tuition, apply for financial aid. If your relatives do come through, their money can help you pay off your financial aid debt.

Don't respond to a college's offer too soon.

Wait until you get all the financial aid packages from all the schools you were accepted to. Your best leverage for a better financial aid deal is a competitive package from a similar-caliber school. The aid package could be used to bargain for a better deal from a school you prefer.

Don't try to figure out loans and financing on your own, unless you have to.

It's best to have help when it comes to something as complicated as loans. Before getting a loan on your own, seek out a financial advisor whose financial counsel you can trust. Ask your parents for a name, or names, of advisors.

Don't be afraid to borrow if you need to.

Sometimes the college experience that's right for you requires taking financial risks. If you're serious about college and can set—and stick to—your goals, it's a wise investment. You're investing in your future.

ALTERNATIVE COLLEGE COST-CUTTING MEASURES

Start with an associate degree.

For students with their hearts set on an elite, expensive school, your best bet may be to attend an affordable school like a community college first. Credits earned at these less-expensive schools can often be transferred to other universities—even the priciest. Spending two years at a community college can cut that tuition in half. For your first two years, they're mostly core classes you'll be taking anyway. So it's the last two years that really count for the college name on the diploma. (Read more about Transferring—the pros, processes, and pitfalls—in Chapter 17.)

Furthermore, by attending a community college and getting an associate degree, you may be able to get a career to pay for college. There are a number of well-paying jobs you can start with a two-year associate degree; registered nurses and dental hygienists are two of them. You can earn your bachelor's degree while you are working.

Get your college credits for less.
To save time and money, consider shaving a year off your undergraduate studies.

There are a number of ways you can earn college credits more inexpensively. Take Advanced Placement and community courses while in high school or obtain college credits through the College-Level Examination Program (CLEP). Another frugal-minded way to earn more college credits is to take classes at community colleges. Students can start taking these classes while they are in high school and continue taking classes during summers when they are in college.

Some three-year degree programs have existed for several years at a number of schools, including Bates College in Maine and Ball State University in Indiana.

Make sure you read Chapter 17 on Transferring Credits.

Graduate in four years.
Surprisingly, most students don't graduate on time. If you graduate on time, you'll save on a fifth or sixth year of college.

Attend a school with a four-year price guarantee.
Some schools offer guarantee plans that promise the same rate for four years. This guarantee protects students from tuition and fee hikes. Schools that have offered this guarantee include the University of Evansville, the University of Kansas, Columbia College in Missouri, and Sewanee: The University of the South. The University of Colorado offers a tuition guarantee for out-of-state students.

Other schools guarantee their students will graduate in four years. If they don't, the school will pay the tuition bill for the next year. Schools that have offered the four-year guarantee include Juniata College, California State Polytechnic University, Green Mountain College, and Western Michigan University.

Become a resident advisor.

Students who posses certain social skills can apply to become a resident advisor (RA). Basically, you will be a student supervisor, peer advisor, and role model for students living in the dorm. RAs usually get their room for free, as well as other benefits.

Qualify for in-state tuition and fees.

The easiest way to do this is to attend a college in the state in which you live. It is generally a lower amount of tuition and fees. For example, if you live in Texas and are going to attend the University of Texas, you would get in-state tuition rate.

Qualify for out-of-state tuition breaks.

Students in nearly every state are eligible to enroll at select out-of-state public colleges and universities at a discount. In fact, many schools offer little-known regional reductions and often require a student or parent to be proactive in applying. Financial need is not a factor in eligibility, but where you live is critical. The program you qualify for depends on what state you permanently reside in.

The country is divided into four regions, and each has a tuition reduction program. Benefits vary by region, state, and school. A couple of states are not eligible; a few states do not participate; some areas and institutions have more stringent guidelines regarding choice of major; others have academic requirements or strict capacity limits; and a few states only offer the reductions to graduate students.

For more information on participating schools, qualifying majors, and application procedures, visit the websites below.

Students in New England

New England Regional Student Program:
http://www.nebhe.org/programs-overview/rsp-tuition-break/overview

Participating states: Connecticut, Maine, Massachusetts, New Hampshire, Rhode Island, and Vermont.

Students in the South
Academic Common Market:
http://www.sreb.org/page/1304/academic_common_market.html

Participating states: Alabama, Arkansas, Delaware, Florida, Georgia, Kentucky, Louisiana, Maryland, Mississippi, North Carolina, Oklahoma, South Carolina, Tennessee, Texas, Virginia, and West Virginia.

Students in the West
Western Undergraduate Exchange: http://wiche.edu/wue

Participating states: Alaska, Arizona, California, Colorado, Hawaii, Idaho, Montana, Nevada, New Mexico, North Dakota, Oregon, South Dakota, Utah, Washington, and Wyoming.

Students in the Midwest
Midwest Student Exchange Program: http://www.mhec.org

Participating states: Illinois, Indiana, Kansas, Michigan, Minnesota, Missouri, Nebraska, North Dakota, and Wisconsin.

Make yourself a local.
You can qualify for in-state tuition if you become a resident of a state. Each state has different resident requirements, but you can typically gain residency by living in a state a year or two before college starts. In addition to living in the state for a certain amount of time, you may also need to take other steps, such as registering to vote, getting a state driver's license, or paying local taxes.

Get a waiver.
Many schools waive out-of-state fees for students who meet specific qualifications like certain standardized test scores or high school GPA.

Work.

Do what many students do and get a part-time job in order to pay for college and the things you need, such as books, housing, and extra- long bed sheets. If you're organized and a go-getter, consider starting your own business.

Work at a college.

Many colleges offer tuition remission to their employees. This means if you work at a school for a certain amount of time, they will give you discounts on tuition. This is also a way to attend a college you might not have gotten into via the regular application process. I had a friend who attended Columbia because she worked there.

Attend a service academy.

There is no tuition or costs to attend a service academy. Additionally, students at these schools receive a small salary. For more information on service academies, see Chapter 15.

Ask for more financial aid.

At some private colleges, you can negotiate on price. It doesn't always work, but it's worth a try. If you decide to do this, know the terminology the college uses. Some prefer the term "appeal." If you choose to ask a school for more financial aid, don't be surprised if they say "no," especially if the school is a competitive one.

Steps in appealing for more aid:

- Honestly evaluate if it's a good financial aid offer. If it's a good offer compared to what the school typically gives, your appeal won't move the needle far.

- Think out the support for your case. Understand why you need more aid. Construct a compelling argument for your need for more financial aid.

- Write an appeals or special circumstances letter. Write an honest and straightforward letter that clearly outlines why you need more financial aid and how you think the school can help you meet your needs.

- Wait. The college needs time to respond.

- Evaluate the results of your appeal.

INTERNATIONAL COLLEGE COUNSELORS TIP: Apply to a financial "safety school." This is a school you and your family will be able to afford without making giant sacrifices.

THE AWARD LETTER

Each school has its own financial aid award letter. Some of these letters are comprehensive and helpful. Others are quite confusing. At times, the letters can even be misleading.

The U.S. Department of Education has been promoting a standard format for all colleges to use, but this is not mandatory yet.

Make sure you fully understand your financial aid package before you accept and sign anything. It is worth seeking help, as needed.

Questions to consider:

- Does the award letter state whether the school is able to meet your full need?

- Is the school offering scholarships, grants, loans, and/or work-study?

- How much of the money must be repaid?

- How much will you be responsible for paying now?

- Will you need a private loan?

- Will you be able to afford the debt at higher interest rates?

Chapter 19:
Scholarships

GET FREE MONEY FOR COLLEGE!

For students who are seniors, juniors, sophomores, and freshmen, whether in public school, private school, or home school, scholarships are available. There are also scholarships for current college students, graduate students, vocational students, older or returning students, veterans, and doctoral candidates. Even if you're an 8th grader reading this, it's not too early to start looking for scholarships. Some scholarships are available for kids as young as six.

Scholarships pay off in more ways than just free money. With certainty, they also look impressively great on your college applications.

What makes scholarships most attractive is that you won't need to repay the money. They're like money trees.

However, even if money grew on trees you'd have to work to get it with a ladder and a basket. The same goes for scholarships. They don't come to you. You have to go out and get them. The good thing is there are a lot of them—many more than there are money trees.

The first step is finding the right scholarships for you. The second step is applying to them.

Joke: Every night a woman prays to win the lottery. One night she says, "God, I pray to win the lottery night after night after night. Why haven't you answered my prayer?"

A flash of light and the voice of G-d booms down from the heavens: "You need to meet me halfway on this. You need to buy a ticket."

MORAL: If you don't try for a scholarship, you won't get one.

Here's a firsthand story on the secret to getting a scholarship, which is APPLYING for a scholarship. At International College Counselors, we have a scholarship for 9th, 10th, and 11th grade students, which we publicize as widely as we can. And, since we work in a high school, we are at least ensured that over 500 students within a certain region know about our scholarship. One year, out of the 500 students, we had ONE application. When a student I did not know approached me in the hall to see if she had won the scholarship, I was able to confidently congratulate her on her win! How did I know she won? I figured if she had asked, she had been our applicant!

To apply to our scholarship, visit http://www.iccscholarship.com.

A SCHOLARSHIP OVERVIEW

Scholarships are available from a variety of sources, including the federal government, state governments, and private sources such as employers, corporations, professional associations, credit unions, local utilities, and educational institutions.

Some scholarships are based on financial needs. Others are awarded to students with special abilities qualified as academic, artistic, or athletic achievement. Still more are reserved for people who have certain religious affiliations, ethnicities, memberships, hobbies, medical conditions, disabilities, or special interests. Some scholarships, like the scholarship essay offered by International College Counselors, require an essay. Others require illustrations, videos, posters, poems, limericks, prom clothes made out of duct tape, or unusual last names. The list goes on and on.

In other words, you don't have to be financially needy to get a scholarship. Nor do you have to have stellar grades.

WHERE TO START YOUR SCHOLARSHIP SEARCH

Students don't have to look farther than their computer to find scholarships to apply to. Several free scholarship databases are available online, offering millions of different scholarships worth billions of dollars.

Some scholarship sites:

- http://www.scholarships.com
- http://www.fastweb.com
- http://www.cappex.com
- Your county school board's website
- Your high school's website

I also recommend searching for scholarships using a web search engine. Include the word "scholarships" in your search keywords and see what comes up. Check Twitter for #scholarship and #scholarships.

HOW TO APPLY FOR SCHOLARSHIPS, AND MORE PLACES TO LOOK FOR THEM

Applying for a scholarship is a lot like applying for college. There are a lot of choices that you must go through in order to put together a list of worthwhile scholarships to spend time on.

Start early.
The more time you put into looking for scholarships, the more choices you'll have. You will also need time to request necessary information and put the materials together. Scholarship requirements may include:

- Transcripts
- Financial aid forms like FAFSA
- Essays
- Letters of recommendation
- Standardized test scores
- Proof of eligibility, such as U.S. Citizenship, birth certificate, or tribal membership card.

Start small.
Local scholarships are easier to get than ones that draw a national applicant pool. Contact your guidance office and check your high school website. Type in the name of your high school, city, state, or county into Google and pair it with the word "scholarship" or "scholarships." Type in the names of local civic groups, your parents' employers, organizations, churches, and local businesses, and pair them with the word "scholarship."

Look for scholarships that fit you.
Are you Hispanic? African American? The child of a single mom? Asthmatic? A descendant of a patriot of the American Revolution? A senior at Botkins High School in Ohio? Were you a golf caddy or a serious ice skater? Are you Jewish, Catholic, Atheistic, Mormon, or Amish? If you've answered " yes" to any of these questions, there is a scholarship for you. The more specific the eligibility requirements, the fewer people will apply.

Use the above websites, an Internet search engine, and the hashtags (#) on Twitter that I mentioned earlier.

Search for scholarships in your field.
If you know what you'd like to study in college—for example, agriculture, automotive, hospitality, health, or parapsychology— type those words into an Internet search engine along with "scholarship." You may be pleasantly surprised. Do this once a week. Scholarships all don't appear at the same time.

Check out the unusual scholarships.
Scholarships can also come with unusual eligibility requirements, such as a scholarship for students who can call ducks. There aren't many of them, but it doesn't hurt to see what may be out there. Start by typing "unusual college scholarships" into the search engine. Then use keyword combinations to match your "specialties" with the word "scholarships." A few examples of the more esoteric scholarships out there:

▸ The Frederick and Mary F. Beckley Scholarship for left-handed students who will be attending Juniata College

- The Tall Clubs International Scholarship for women who are at least 5'10" and men who are at least 6'2"

- The Little People of America Scholarship for those 4'10" or less in height

- Zolp Scholarships for students at Loyola University who are Catholic and whose last name is Zolp

- The Duck Brand Duct Tape " Stuck on Prom" Contest, which requires entrants to attend a high school prom wearing complete attire or accessories made from duct tape

- The National Make It Yourself With Wool (NMIYWW) competition awarding scholarships for knitting wool garments

- The STARFLEET Academy Scholarship offering several scholarships for active members of the Starfleet Academy. (You need to be a member for at least a year. So, if you're a sophomore reading this, think about joining now.)

Check each specific college's scholarships.

Many colleges offer full-tuition academic scholarships. School-specific scholarships, where a student can usually receive the largest amount of scholarship aid, are typically given to top athletes, top test score recipients, and other outstanding students. In order to apply for these scholarships, you need to contact each school individually. A rule of thumb is that if you are in the top 25 percent of the admitted class, there could be some scholarship money waiting for you. So a student who can get into MIT with no scholarship money may receive a full ride at Georgia Tech (still a great school!), and a student who can get into Penn could get a full ride at Drexel (a terrific option!).

Don't obsess about the big-money dream.

Ideally you'd get your tuition paid with one big scholarship. But realistically, the prestigious, big-money scholarships receive more than 100,000 applications each year just because they are the most lucrative. The more money attached to the scholarship, the more well known they'll usually be. However, if you are truly qualified to be in the running for even the most competitive of scholarships, don't let the opportunity pass you by. Go for it.

Look for "renewable" scholarships.
A $500 renewable scholarship may not sound like much at first, but over four years it totals $2,000.

Determine whether you are a realistic candidate.
Don't waste your time. Carefully filter scholarships during your search. You should only apply to the ones that match your skills, heritage, area code, or other qualifications. Scholarships are very strict on this.

Apply to only one or two scholarships at a time.
Make the scholarship search more manageable. Give one or two scholarships your all before moving on to the next ones. If you spread your efforts too thin, it will show. This is not to say you should apply for only two scholarships. Set a goal. Give yourself two weeks for two scholarships and move on to the next.

Do the research.
See who has won in the past and make it your job to understand why they won. You can't copy what they've done, but chances are you will need to be in the same ballpark in order to be a contender. If you are falling way short of what the past winners offered, the scholarship is not for you. For example, you will not win a scholarship based on community service if you only have a smattering of volunteer work on your resume.

Stay organized.
Make separate folders for each scholarship and keep track of what is needed. Track the scholarships on a calendar and make triple sure deadlines aren't missed.

YOU HAVE A SCHOLARSHIP APPLICATION. NOW WHAT?

Follow the instructions <u>carefully</u>.
To the letter. Count the words on the essay and provide the right materials. If you have any questions about what the scholarship requirements are, or how to fill out a part of the application, call or email the scholarship sponsors. Many applications are eliminated because the directions were not followed to the letter.

Stay on topic in the essay/video.
If the essay asks for the philosophic themes of an Ayn Rand novel, don't be clever by comparing her to Batman. Give them what they asked for. Don't give more. Don't give less. Make sure any scholarship application materials or correspondences position you as someone worthy and deserving of the scholarship.

Check and recheck and recheck the application.
Words must be spelled right and all the questions answered. Make sure it's signed and dated by the right people, for example, by a teacher if that is what the application requests. And make sure all the words can be easily read.

Send the application in on time.
Make sure you do this!

LAST-CHANCE SCHOLARSHIPS

Life is full of surprises, and there are students who will back out of their commitment to a school. This usually happens during the summer, before college starts.

Occasionally, the financial aid set aside for these students will be redistributed. If you want to put yourself in the running to receive these funds, you must be proactive.

Contact the schools in the middle of the summer.

This is when they'll be able to tell you just how much, if any, financial aid there is for the taking.

Research scholarship options.

The rules applying to the dispersal of one scholarship may be different than those of another, even at the same school. Determine which of the school's scholarships that you might be qualified for and call the financial aid office to see which ones might still be available late in the summer.

Sell yourself.

Be sure to point out if you boosted your GPA during the latter half of your senior year, a time when many students cruise to the finish line rather than sprint.

Be super nice.

Being polite and professional can't guarantee you'll receive funding, but doing the opposite will almost certainly guarantee you won't see an extra dime.

Try again later.

You never know who will be transferring, dropping out, or kicked out for behavioral or academic issues. The winter is a good time to ask again.

INTERNATIONAL COLLEGE COUNSELORS TIP: If you are seeking more financial aid, get a job if you don't already have one. We've seen aid officials give extra credit to students who are doing all they can to make ends meet before they seek more financial aid.

SCHOLARSHIPS DO AFFECT FINANCIAL AID PACKAGES

Contact the financial aid office of any colleges you are considering to find out the details. Each school has its own policy on which types of aid may be reduced or eliminated by the scholarship money. Different types of aid that may be affected by scholarship monies are loans, work-study, and need-based grants. But, please don't use this as a reason not to apply for scholarships. Here's why:

- A bird in the hand is worth two in the bush. In other words, take what you can get!

- Scholarship awards (the fact that you won them) are prestigious and look good on college applications.

Beware of the scholarship scams.

- If it sounds too good to be true, it probably is.

- Never pay an application fee.

- If you are considering a legitimate scholarship site or scholarship, you will not be asked to pay any money to apply or receive details. The fee can be as low as $5, but don't do it.

Look up the organization offering the scholarship.
Scams often misuse the names of legitimate government and nonprofit organizations. They may also be using words like "national," "federal," "foundation," or "administration." A ".org" website does not make a scholarship automatically legitimate.

Don't get taken.
If you receive unsolicited mail telling you you've won a scholarship, but you need to send money to claim it, throw the letter away. You won't get thousands, but you will lose money. Another scam will send a check made out to you. In order to cash that check, they will say you need to send them money. Don't send them any money—you won't see any money from them.

Don't pay for what you can get free.
Some scholarship-matching services claim they will help match you with scholarships—for a fee. Before you sign on, do a search of your own for free at sites like http://www.fastweb.com and http://www.finaid.org and via Google and Twitter search. Many of those paid matching services will send you a list similar to those you can find yourself. Check the free scholarship sites first.

INTERNATIONAL COLLEGE COUNSELORS TIP: If a scholarship-matching service "guarantees" success or scholarships, don't use it. Nobody can guarantee that you'll win a scholarship.

Signs of a scam:

▸ Mention of high success rates or "free money"

▸ No website or telephone number

▸ A post-office box for a return address

▸ Time pressure for a quick reply

▸ Notification by phone

The Sales Pitch That's Not a Scholarship

"Congratulations on being nominated to attend the National Young Leaders Conference in Washington, D.C.," reads the fancy script on the expensive-feeling card complete with gold seal. The card promises a "lifetime advantage" and valuable resume padding. It's hard to miss the words "elite," "college," "distinguished," and "select."

The letter's claim that this program is a huge honor and will distinguish you as a college applicant is simply not true. These particular leadership conferences won't enhance your college applications any more or less than that art club you joined at your high school.

You may meet other kids who are interested in government, attend workshops, hear speakers, and sightsee, but getting invited isn't an "honor." College admissions officers and college advisors are aware that attendance for most students depends on their zip code and ability to pay.

Companies in this business include/have included: the National Student Leadership Conference, People to People Ambassador Programs, Leadership Classroom, Envision, and the Congressional Youth Leadership Council.

SCHOLARSHIPS FOR NON-U.S. CITIZENS

U.S. citizens who live abroad are eligible for federal and school scholarships.

If you are an international or undocumented student, your best source of scholarships (and financial aid) will be the college you attend. Although not all, some colleges have scholarship programs specifically for non-U.S. citizens.

If you don't live in the United States, you can look at a college's website to see what aid is available to international students. Each school has different funding. Some set aside money for students from specific countries, some are open to students worldwide, and some require that you study a certain field. If you are confused about the money you qualify for, call the college and ask to speak with a college admissions officer or financial aid expert.

If you are accepted into more than one college, you may be able to use offered scholarships and financial aid to negotiate a better deal from your first choice of college.

Most general scholarship websites do not list the scholarships or have very limited listings for international students, but one that does is http://www.iefa.org.

If you're a non-U.S. citizen, you really should make sure you read this whole chapter. It's important to know that you should never have to pay to find or apply for scholarships. If you're ever asked for a credit card or other financial information before you can use a scholarship search engine, seek scholarships elsewhere. There are a number of free search engines that I've listed. No one can guarantee you will get a scholarship either, so don't pay anyone who says they can GUARANTEE you get one.

No matter where you're from, there are likely opportunities specific to you whether they're related to your country or something you do. Read the early part of this chapter for more details!

Chapter 20:
Free and Inexpensive Schools

Public school students who are not accustomed to paying for school might be thrilled to learn that a free or very reduced- price college education is available from some very unique colleges, both brick and mortar and online. A number of them offer free tuition regardless of a student's financial situation and/or accept international students. Some examples include:

Deep Springs College: http://www.deepsprings.edu/home
Deep Springs offers an associate degree in the liberal arts. Each student attends for two years and receives a full scholarship valued at over $50,000 per year. The school is exceptionally small with a student body of twenty-six. Only ten to fifteen students per year are admitted. Deep Springs operates on the belief that manual labor and political deliberation are integral parts of a comprehensive liberal arts education. Students of the college work each day on the school's cattle ranch, alfalfa farm, and garden in California's High Desert.

The Williamson Free School of Mechanical Trades:
http://www.williamson.edu
Williamson offers Associate in Specialized Technology Degrees in carpentry, masonry, horticulture, landscaping and turf management, machine tool technology, paint and coatings technology, and power plant technology. All approximately 250 students attend on full scholarships that cover tuition, room, board, and textbooks. The campus is located in Delaware County, Pennsylvania.

College of the Ozarks: http://www.cofo.edu
College of the Ozarks focuses on providing a free Christian education to good students who demonstrate financial need. The college was founded to serve students specifically from the Ozarks region, though it occasionally admits students from outside the region.

Full-time students must work fifteen hours each week at an assigned campus workstation, which can include a hotel, computer center, fire department, water treatment plant, cafeteria, pool, fruitcake and jelly kitchen, grist mill, museum, theatre, and radio station.

Alice Lloyd College: http://www.alc.edu
At Alice Lloyd College, tuition is guaranteed to full-time students. These students must work from ten to twenty hours each week in a variety of work areas as a condition for graduation. Alice Lloyd emphasizes the integration of Christian principles in every aspect of campus life. The eastern Kentucky campus is located in the center of Appalachia.

Berea College: http://www.berea.edu
Students admitted to Berea receive a four-year tuition scholarship that covers 100 percent of tuition costs for four years of enrollment. Laptop computers are provided to every enrolled student. One of the admission requirements is financial need. The campus is located in Berea, Kentucky.

The Curtis Institute of Music: http://www.curtis.edu
The Curtis Institute of Music provides full-tuition scholarships to all of its students regardless of their financial situation. Applicants must audition in person. According to the Curtis website, enrollment is limited to the number of musicians needed for a symphony orchestra, opera department, and select programs in piano, composition, conducting, organ, guitar, and harpsichord (approximately 165 students). The school is located in Philadelphia.

Webb Institute: http://www.webb.edu
Webb offers one academic option, a double major in Naval Architecture and Marine Engineering. Located in Glen Cove, NY, it's a full-tuition scholarship private program. In addition to the full-tuition scholarship, Webb students are eligible to apply for additional school scholarships.

Franklin W. Olin College of Engineering: http://www.olin.edu
Every admitted student receives a half-tuition merit scholarship valued at more than $80,000 over eight semesters. Admission to Olin is need-blind.

Western Governors University: http://www.wgu.edu

WGU is an online university that charges tuition at a flat rate every six months, so you pay for the time, not the credit hours. If you can complete your program in less time by taking more classes in any given semester, you only pay tuition for the time it takes. In other words, the faster you progress, the more money you can save.

William E. Macaulay Honors College at CUNY:

http://www.macaulay.cuny.edu

Each Macaulay student is awarded a full-tuition merit scholarship. Students are selected for their high school records and leadership potential. Macaulay students can enroll in any one of the seven City University of New York (CUNY) colleges. All Macaulay students also receive a laptop computer; a $7,500 Opportunities Fund to pursue global research, service, and internships; and a Cultural Passport to NY arts and cultural venues.

Chapter 21:
Tips For High School Student Athletes

The talented high school athlete's top question is: How do I get recruited?

My answer: An athlete needs to get noticed by the right school and coach. This means the ones that fit your needs and abilities.

Getting noticed is certainly easier in some sports and cities. Athletes in AAAAA and AAAA football and baseball in some states have scouts who show up regularly to their games. If you've ever seen the TV show *Friday Night Lights*, you'll know that for some sports, and in some cities, thousands of people come to games. Then, too, many sports are regularly covered in widely distributed newspapers or newscasts. Cross-country, track, swimming, softball, golf, and other sports are often included in this group.

But, every year, thousands of other outstanding athletes are overlooked for one simple reason: the coaches didn't know they were out there.

Don't make the mistake of expecting your high school coach to get you a scholarship. Most of them don't have the time or the resources. If you want a college scholarship and athletic opportunities, you must do a lot of work on your own or with the help of a counselor, parent, or guardian.

Have a power drink and take a deep breath. Whether you participate in baseball, basketball, bowling, cross- country, fencing, field hockey, football, golf, gymnastics, ice hockey, lacrosse, rowing, skiing, soccer, softball, swimming and diving, tennis, track and field, softball, volleyball, water polo, or wrestling, there are ways that you can help yourself be recruited.

HOW TO GET RECRUITED

Watch this video: http://www.freerecruitingwebinar.org
The Free Recruiting Webinar, operated by the 501(c)(3) non-profit Recruiting Education Foundation, Inc., is designed to educate athletes and parents on the recruiting process. In approximately one hour, it addresses many important recruiting topics, including Scholarship Myths and Facts, the NCAA and NAIA Eligibility Centers, NCAA Core Course Requirements, National Letter of Intent, Finding the Right School, and much more.

Contact coaches.
Depending on your sport, start contacting coaches at schools of interest and building relationships with them as early as possible. The goal is to get coaches and recruiters to know your name in a good way. For example, send them some newspaper articles about you and the teams you play for, or a link to a particularly spectacular achievement. If there is an opportunity to meet a coach, go and introduce yourself with a quick rundown of your best achievements. You may ask them the best way to showcase your talents. Some will request videos; some will have camps; some will want a resume. Finding out early is the key to meeting the coach's needs.

Create a resume.
Highlight your athletic and academic achievements. Keep track of all your meets, tournaments, and achievements to display on the resume. Specifically you want to write down:

- All your statistics, including goals, hits, assists, blocks, runs, or whatever else is measured in your sport

- Your best times, heights, scores, etc. if you're an athlete who competes in a sport with a matrix, like track and field, cross country, swimming or bowling

- Your individual and team's wins and losses

- Awards, including MVP, Most Improved, Scholar Athlete, Most Defensive Player, etc.

Make a sports video of yourself in action.
This direction is for athletes who compete in sports without a measurable matrix. There is a real probability that a college coach will never see you play in real life until you play for him or her. The best video is a combination game video and skills video. You want to keep it relatively short (about five minutes) and put your best highlights first. Don't forget to include your contact information—your name, school, phone number, and email address. Consider setting up a channel for yourself on YouTube or posting your video on an athletic recruiting website.

Get into the Internet zone.
Visit college sports sites and college sites and collect as much information about the different sports programs as you can. You're looking for a school that will be a good fit for you and your talents, athletically and academically.

Get evaluated (if you can).
Many third-party people serve as the eyes and ears of the coaches who don't have time to see every player. Get to know the evaluators in your area. Coaches and evaluators face immense pressure to fill their slots with the most gifted athletes they can find. Their jobs depend on it. Your proactivity actually can make their job easier from their perspective.

Attend college sports camps (if you can).
The director of the camp is usually the college head coach. Take these camps seriously and use them as opportunities to showcase your talents.

Keep up your grades.
With the exception of big-time college football and basketball, other sports do not typically offer full-athletic scholarships for budgetary reasons. However, colleges do offer what's called merit money. This is where grades come into play. If you have good grades, a college can offer you a half-athletic scholarship as well as a half-merit scholarship based on grades. This can equal a full scholarship.

Do well on the SAT or ACT and take them early.
For the same reason as the above.

INTERNATIONAL COLLEGE COUNSELORS TIP: If a college does show interest in you, answer any request they have immediately. If a coach or school is requesting more information, chances are you are probably being seriously considered. Ask your high school coach to complete any requests for information about you as soon as possible.

A BRIEF FOUR-YEAR TIMELINE

Freshmen
Take this year to grow and develop your skills. Also, plan your academic calendar. You want to make sure you meet the academic eligibility at the end of your high school career. Even a high school sports superstar will not be eligible to play as a college freshman if he or she does not have a transcript with the right high school courses. Athletes and parents of athletes, make sure you read the NCAA Guide for the College Bound Student Athlete. A free PDF to download can be found at http://www.ncaastudent.org.

Sophomores
Get serious if you are interested in competing in college. Start working on raising your visibility and building a reputation as a mature, hard-working team player. This is also the year you should start researching the ins and outs of recruiting, regulations, colleges, coaches, and sports programs.

Juniors
This year is your most important one. It is the accomplishments of your junior year that will get the recruiting phone calls later in the year. Talk to your coach about serving as captain of your team; if it doesn't work junior year, you can try again senior year. Get on the college coaches' radar screens as soon as possible to better your chances of successfully getting recruited. Boost your visibility by reaching out to coaches with notes and calls, visiting schools and meeting coaches. Don't get

181

discouraged if you don't hear from coaches. NCAA rules prevent them from contacting or calling you until late in your junior year.

Seniors

Make sure that you are eligible by completing all the classes you need for academic eligibility. Show continuing development in your sports skills. Don't slack off until after you've received and signed the "Letter of Intent"—and even then, if you really mess up, they can drop you.

INTERNATIONAL COLLEGE COUNSELORS TIP: Take care of your body and keep working hard to get stronger, faster, and fitter. It's a competitive environment out there—but if you're a true athlete at heart, knowing that should only push you more.

Chapter 22:
Independent College Advisors

Public school counselors in the U.S. have an average caseload of about 450 students. In many high schools, students have the opportunity to see their college guidance counselor only once a year. One time. In the entire year.

To make matters worse, budget cuts are forcing some counselors to spend even less time with students and more time on other unrelated responsibilities, like handling discipline issues, supervising the cafeteria at lunch, or proctoring exams.

In contrast, counselors in private schools have a median caseload of approximately 100 students.

As a student of a public high school, you probably are not surprised by these figures.

While I've rarely met a high school counselor who has not done a high-quality, professional job, needless to say, the numbers make life difficult. Apart from petitioning your local politician and school headmaster, what is a public school student to do?

Many families have turned to working with a private college counselor. It's a trend that's been on the rise. As other students you're competing against are hiring independent advisors, I did want to mention what to look out for if you're considering hiring someone.

Independent college advisors can be of enormous value, if used correctly.

VALUE OF INDEPENDENT COLLEGE ADVISORS

Primarily, independent college advisors provide you with the individualized attention you need to properly tackle the college admissions process. This is about you—the individual—and finding the best fit for you.

A good college advisor will help you with your college selection and the application process. Some parts of the admission process include: help with high school planning; refinement of extracurricular and academic interests; essay advice and review of essays; interview preparation; exploration of financial aid and scholarships; and wait- list and deferral strategies.

Additionally, independent advisors help relieve stress and maximize results.

CHOOSING AN INDEPENDENT COLLEGE ADVISOR

Like in any field, there are individuals who are good and others who are not. Many people moonlight as college advisors or are "experts" because they just helped their daughter/son/friend get into their top choice. Others have questionable ethical standards.

In choosing an independent college advisor, I recommend looking for these factors:

Professional Memberships
All independent college advisors should belong to at least one professional organization like the National Association for College Admission Counseling (NACAC) or the Independent Educational Consultants Association (IECA). These organizations are for serious professionals. For both of these organizations, the member must have at least three years of professional experience, have worked with multiple students, and have their application approved by a committee.

Credentials
Review the college counselors' credentials. Does the advisor have a bachelor's degree from an accredited institution? Does the advisor have at least three years of experience as a college advisor? Has the advisor previously placed students in the Ivy League or top-tier schools? If so, how many and where? If the advisor has only placed students in state schools, this may not be a good fit for you. Does the advisor use a web-based college research tool like Naviance to track former

184

students—their grades, scores, and other variables to compare them to you?

Keeps Current

Advisors should be meeting with admissions representatives, visiting colleges, going to workshops, reading up on trends, and fully immersed in college admissions. Your English teacher may be an excellent writer and proofreader, but do they really know what's trending on essays and what the admissions representatives want to see?

Team Approach

With over 4,500 colleges, not every college counselor can know everything about each school. Look for a company that shares resources on schools, admissions strategies, and college contacts. The team approach is also beneficial when it comes time to reviewing essays. Does the company have someone who does a second review? Even the best editors miss mistakes, so it's always better to have a few eyes reading over the essays.

Ethical Standards

College advisors should observe the highest legal and moral standards. A college advisor should not write your college essay, guarantee admission into a certain school, or help fudge information on a transcript. Additionally, similar to how colleges perform Internet searches on students, you should do a search on your advisor or the company. If the first thing that comes up is something about questionable behavior, you may want to look elsewhere.

Time and Communication

Your independent advisor should be available when it's convenient for you, within reason. Are they available after school, on the weekends, and when school is off? Are they available via Skype, phone, and email? Is this their full-time position, or do they dabble in college advising?

QUESTIONS TO ASK INDEPENDENT COLLEGE ADVISORS

Think about what's most important to you when hiring an independent advisor. This person is going to be helping you with one of the biggest decisions of your life. Some questions you may want to consider:

- Do you belong to any professional associations? If so, which ones?
- How do you keep up with trends?
- How often do you visit colleges or meet with admissions officers?
- Do you attend professional conferences or training?
- How long have you been in business as an independent college advisor?
- What is your experience in college advising?
- Is college advising your full-time profession?
- Have you placed students in Ivy League/top-tier schools? If so, which ones?
- At which grade in school do you start working with a student? (You really want one who starts with students in at least the 9th grade.)
- Do you work alone, or do you have colleagues to work in a team approach?
- What type of web-based college research tools do you use?
- What type of services do you offer, and how much do you charge for your services?
- Do you offer hourly or comprehensive packages?
- Will you meet or Skype with me initially for free?
- How do you communicate with students? Do you keep parents included in communication?
- How do you measure a student's success?

You should ask these additional questions to check for scammers. If they say yes, look elsewhere!

- Do you guarantee admission into a school?

- Do you guarantee scholarship money?

- Will you write the college essay?

- Do you accept any form of compensation from a school in exchange for placement?

- Are there any additional fees other than what is on the contract?

INTERNATIONAL COLLEGE COUNSELORS TIP: Similar to picking the right college, you want to click with the advisor and make sure he or she understands your goals. We recommend signing up with an advisor who will meet with you first before you sign on the dotted line.

Chapter 23:
The Application is In.
Don't Relax Yet.

SIGNS, SYMPTOMS, AND DANGERS OF SENIORITIS

Symptoms: Laziness. Skipping classes. Failing to study hard for tests or write coherent papers. Disinterest in school-related academics and activities.

Diagnosis: Senioritis.

Prescription: Graduation.

Avoid the epidemic. Don't catch senioritis. Slacking off in your senior year may seem like something you feel you deserve, but chances are you'll do yourself more harm than good.

One, you'll miss out on a half-year worth of learning. This will leave you less prepared for college.

Two, college admissions officers really do pay attention to what you've accomplished in your senior year. They look at your grades and your activities and, in some cases, your more recent Facebook posts.

The temptation to blow off school and all the work involved is especially strong when students have already been accepted into college.

But, did you notice if your college application package included a form called the "mid-year grade report"? Your counselor will fill it out and send it off to your college when the time comes, and it will become part of your full admissions evaluation.

Colleges do have the right to block your admission, and students do get booted. Read your college acceptance letters carefully. Many times colleges include clear warnings to students, informing them that admission is contingent on successful performance throughout senior year.

The number of students who get their acceptance offers withdrawn is small, as the drop usually needs to be significant before colleges go that far. However, colleges can and do punish in other ways. A student may receive a harsh letter warning them to get it together. Or he or she may need to explain, in a letter or a phone call, what happened with their academic performance. A drop in performance can also result in consequences such as getting dropped from an honors program or having your admissions postponed. These situations are not as rare as you may think.

Generally, the more selective the college, the more weight is put on what you do in your last semester.

INTERNATIONAL COLLEGE COUNSELORS TIP: We always recommend sending update letters to colleges about a month after your application has been sent. In this way, you can reiterate interest, update the school on new accomplishments, and allow the school to see that you are a serious student.

Don't plan on doing anything really stupid, no matter where you plan to go to college. Colleges regularly rescind admissions offers from students who get arrested or suspended from school for unlawful or prohibited activities like drinking.

Don't plan on dropping any courses. Even substituting an online course for one you're taking at school will raise red flags with a college admissions office. Admission offers have been revoked because colleges see a dropped course as significant underperformance, especially if the student drops a rigorous course. It's really not worth it.

My sincere recommendation is to take preventative care. Senioritis may not be curable, but it is treatable: Stay active. Stay involved. Stay focused. Stay on your regular schedules. Take a college course to get yourself more prepared for college. The credit may even count at your school, and that's one less class you'll need to take.

You have done most of the hard work, and it would be foolish to let all that hard work go to waste now. You also have a whole summer to goof off if that's what you want to do in between filling out the dorm room papers and shopping for bean bag chairs.

Chapter 24:
College Responses and Decision Making

When high school seniors know that the notification date is near, there is little a student can do to lessen the anxiety. Chances are moms, dads, counselors, teachers and even principals are feeling anxious themselves.

Even if you get into your first choice college, this will probably be a hard time for you. You're hardly alone. After the initial euphoria, most students start thinking about what going to college really means.

For students who get rejected, this may be the first time they're dealing with major disappointment. Don't let this damage your self-esteem.

Feel your emotions and think them through.

THE MANY POTENTIAL OUTCOMES OF YOUR COLLEGE APPLICATION

Acceptance/Admittance
Yay! You've been admitted to the school to start in the fall of the next year, as long as you don't do anything truly drastic. Don't let your grades drop significantly or get arrested, among other things. Schools have the right to withdraw their acceptance. If you have been accepted, you typically have until May 1 to submit your deposit to secure your place at a school.

Deferral
A deferral is different than being wait-listed. A deferral means that a student who applied Early Action or Early Decision is being considered as a regular applicant. You've neither been accepted nor denied; your application was rolled over into the regular decision pool. Given that the school can only admit a limited number of applicants per semester, the school wants to compare you to the students that apply for regular decision. If you are deferred, it can always help if you show additional interest in the college. See my advice below on How to Handle a Deferral.

Denial

This means you have not been accepted to the school. Don't take it personally, and read my advice below on Your Response to the Admissions Decisions.

Wait-List

This means quite literally you're on a wait-list. The schools know you exist, but you're not a first-choice applicant. Whether or not you get off the wait-list and into the school depends on how many accepted students decide to attend the school. If you're wait-listed and really want to go to your first-choice college, you may have to make a deposit at another school as an insurance policy. While bad for students, wait-lists are good for colleges. Wait-lists allow them to ensure that they have enough students to fill all of their spaces. Send the school any new updates that can enhance your application.

Conditional Admittance

Select applicants who do not meet the minimum admissions requirements but show potential for success may get a conditional admittance. This means the school wants you, but you need to fulfill other requirements before they fully admit you. If you get one of these, the school will let you know what you need to do—for example, complete a summer/special program, or take certain classes your freshman year.

Spring or Summer Admittance

Sometime a student is accepted on the condition he or she starts classes in a term other than the fall. Students can inquire if the school offers academic options, study-abroad programs, or other opportunities to fill the time gap. Other students use the gap time to take courses at a community college, work, or travel. Schools do this because there is additional room on campus in the spring and summer semesters, when students study abroad or are on summer break.

Guaranteed Transfer or Deferred Admission

This means the college recognizes your potential but doesn't believe your record is strong enough to admit you right away. Typically the letters say that if you attend another university for a year and maintain a certain GPA, they will guarantee you a transfer spot sophomore year. There are a number of colleges that offer and have offered this option, including Cornell, the State University of New York System, Middlebury College in Vermont, and the University of Maryland. If you really have your heart set on a school, ask about this option. Some colleges do not advertise that they offer deferred admission.

YOUR RESPONSE TO THE ADMISSIONS DECISIONS

Typically, a deferral means the college wants to compare you with the full applicant pool because your application did not shine enough for them to admit you early.

Unlike a rejection, a deferral offers hope and chance. Ironically, hope is not always the least stressful option. You have work to do if you want to improve your chances of turning the "maybe" into a "yes."

Here are some suggestions:

▸ Don't panic.

▸ If possible, try to find the reason you weren't accepted straightaway.

Get information.
Contact the admissions office and see if you can find out why you were deferred. Then ask for suggestions regarding turning your deferral into an acceptance. By doing this, you'll make the school aware of your commitment and get more information. Do not call if the college has specifically asked that students not call them.

Send in improved standardized test scores.
This is especially important if you believe your submitted scores may not have measured up.

Send in your midyear grades if the college asks for them.
Make sure you meet their deadline. (This is another reason why it's important not to let your grades slide.)

Write a letter.
Sincerely express your continued interest in the school and reasons why you believe it would be a good match for you. Do not come across as whiny or negative. Be yourself; sound personal; be interesting; and be positive. Attach information about any new and meaningful accomplishments that are not in your original application. Accomplishments could include new activities, new awards, or leadership positions.

Send in a strong and relevant additional recommendation.
The best letter of recommendation would discuss your unique qualities and why they make you an ideal match for a school. What you don't want to do is send a generic recommendation. Make sure you check to see if the college allows you to send extra letters before you send them.

Let go.
There is no one "perfect" school. Hope for the best, but prepare to go to one of your backup schools.

INTERNATIONAL COLLEGE COUNSELORS TIP: At all times while communicating with the college, be polite, concise, professional, positive, and enthusiastic. Don't express frustration or anger or try to convince the school they made a mistake.

DEFERRAL LETTERS THAT WORK BEST

Letters of appeal work best if you can give the college more reason to reconsider you—for example, a new honor or significant achievement. Also important in the letter are a few lines that reaffirm your interest in the school. And don't forget to thank the admissions officer!

Sample Deferral Letter 1

Dear Mr. Garcia,

Although my admission for Early Action has been deferred, I am still very interested in Binghamton and would very much like to be admitted, and therefore I wish to keep you up to date on my activities and achievements.

Earlier this month I participated in the 2013 Siemens Competition in Math, Science & Technology in New York City. My high school team was awarded a $10,000 scholarship for our research on graph theory. The judges consisted of a panel of scientists and mathematicians led by former astronaut Dr. Thomas Jones.

The awards were presented at a ceremony on December 7. Over two thousand students entered this competition, and I was extremely honored to be recognized alongside the other winners. More information on this competition can be found through the Siemens Foundation web site: http://www.siemensfoundation.org/en/.

Thank you for your continued consideration of my application.

Sincerely,

Name
High School
Application ID

Sample Deferral Letter 2

Dear Ms. Davis,

Last week I learned that my application for early decision at Johns Hopkins was deferred. As you can imagine, this news was disappointing to me—Johns Hopkins remains the university I'm most excited about attending. I visited a lot of schools during my college search, and Johns Hopkins's program in International Studies appeared to be a perfect match for my interests and aspirations.

I want to thank you and your colleagues for the time you put into considering my application. After I applied for early decision, I received a couple more pieces of information that I hope will strengthen my application. First, I retook the SAT in November, and my combined score went from 1990 to 2200. The College Board will be sending you an official score report soon. Also, I was recently elected to be the Captain of our school Ski Team, a group of twenty-eight students who compete in regional competitions. As Captain, I will have a central role in the team's scheduling, publicity, and fundraising. I have asked the team's coach to send you a supplemental letter of recommendation that will address my role within the Ski Team.

Many thanks for your consideration,

Name
High School
Application ID

HOW TO DEAL WITH DISAPPOINTMENT

Talk it out.
If you are rejected from your first choice college, find a trusted adult with whom you can vent your emotions. You need to accept that you didn't get in and move forward with the opportunities that do present themselves. If you have been rejected, some schools do offer opportunities for appeal, but these are rarely successful unfortunately. While getting into your first-pick college is important, if you don't, it's

not the end of the world. You shouldn't love or like yourself any less. The world is not coming to an end. College is one step on a long road. Sure it's a big step, but it's not the final destination.

Add up what really counts.

The college admissions officers are looking at numbers: a GPA, an SAT score, and the number of applicants that year. Numbers have little to do with you as a good person. Besides, it's too late now to change the numbers, so beating yourself up isn't going to make anything better.

Remember the subjectivity factor.

Much of the college admission process is out of your control. While I do believe admissions officers try to be fair and thorough, college admissions are subjective, perhaps even more than most students and parents realize. High scores aren't the only thing that counts. Subjectivity comes into play as admissions officers compare the applications. Maybe the band really needed a new flugelhorn player. Perhaps the school does not need another rhythmic gymnast. Sometimes the numbers just don't work in your favor.

Celebrate the acceptances.

Celebrate the college acceptance letters that you do get. Getting into any college is something to celebrate.

Consider additional applications.

Even as late as April and May, some colleges are still accepting applications. Wish you had applied to a particular school? Now is the time to see if they still have space.

INTERNATIONAL COLLEGE COUNSELORS TIP: The Common Application allows you to sort by deadline. Don't be afraid to apply to colleges towards the end of your senior year.

Remember you can always transfer.

Our recommendation is to keep this as a back pocket option and not as a goal. If you go to a college with the intent of transferring, you won't be able to enjoy the full college experience you can have. Many students find that once they settle in, they're actually very happy.

I promise, no matter what happens: after the madness, there will be a calm.

ACCEPTANCE! DECISION-MAKING AFTER THE "THICK ENVELOPES" (THESE DAYS, THEY USUALLY TELL YOU BY EMAIL)

The envelopes are in, the emails have been opened, and the web portals have been read.

If you have more than one acceptance in your hand, you're in the driver's seat. The colleges have taken their sweeeeet time choosing you, and now it's your turn to choose them. They've given you the month of April to make your choice. Far beyond the glossy paper of the brochures, here are some things you should consider:

Economics
It's hard to deny that this may be a factor for many students. If you've been offered a generous financial aid package or a scholarship, it's going to be hard to ignore this "bonus." However, the price tag may not be so much a factor in some cases. Some families have the funds, and some schools have the funding. In fact, Ivies and a small number of other schools across the country have policies that will meet the full financial need of students and allow them to attend irrespective of their ability to pay.

What you need to do with any offer is carefully review it. Look at the tuition and the amount and type of financial aid you were offered. Go back and read Chapter 18 on Financial Aid.

Fit
Where do you feel like you will fit in best? Some students thrive at universities where the city itself plays an important role in one's overall education. Cities included on this list include New York, Boston, New

198

Orleans, and Los Angeles. The cultural and internship opportunities can also be enormous. However, city schools tend to be more impersonal, and cities aren't as conducive to a school community atmosphere. Residential campus schools like Dartmouth College in Hanover, New Hampshire or Williams College in Williamstown, Massachusetts, pride themselves on providing everything you need right there on campus, from cultural activities to social life. They have more of a community atmosphere.

In order to figure out fit, you should ideally visit the school. It's the only way you'll get a real feel for the location and the culture. On campus, try to speak with professors and students.

If you can't visit, try to talk to current students, recent alumni, or admissions officers.

Academics

Do you have an idea of what you want to do in the future? Ideally, you should have a vague idea of the career path you want to pursue, and you need a school that offers a major or program that will allow you to explore that option to its fullest. For example, if you know you want to go to medical school when you graduate, make sure there's an undergrad program strong in math and sciences courses.

Also be aware that there can be real differences in the course of study at various places. Some schools like Columbia University and the University of Chicago require students to take a core curriculum. The mandatory courses can take up to two years to complete. Open curriculum schools, like Brown and Amherst have no required courses. Instead they require that students take one of a list of first- year seminars. Guidelines and advisors at these schools help students with their course choices.

I also recommend you research the professors and special opportunities at different schools. The University of Michigan College of Engineering, for example, creates partnerships between first- and second-year students and UM faculty and research scientists.

Culture

At some schools, like the University of North Carolina, the culture revolves around sports. At others it could be academics, religion, or a certain industry. At the University of Southern California, for example, the entertainment industry seems to have a permanent presence no matter what students are studying. At New York University, the city is a center of life. The key to the culture is students. Talk to the students. They can tell you what the school is really like. What are the dorms like? What does everyone do on Friday or Saturday nights?

Job Connections

After college you'll want to get a job, so it's smart to consider a college's career services center. Call them and ask about job fairs, internship opportunities, on-campus corporate interviews, and the number of students per career counselor.

INTERNATIONAL COLLEGE COUNSELORS TIP: Only you will know what is truly important to you. I suggest you create a list of all the questions you want answered and then go visit the school. If you've already visited the schools, then visit your top two choices again. Take a good hard look at the school. Can you see yourself fitting into the culture? Do you feel comfortable? This is going to be your home away from home for the next four years.

Specific questions you may want to ask if you haven't already: How hard is it to get into the classes I want? How small or big are the classes? Are there internships, and how does the school help students prepare for life after college? Does the school provide career placement or help with graduate and professional programs? Does the school offer the athletic opportunities I'd want to participate in or cheer for? What will it mean to be an alumnus of the University of Miami rather than Miami University?

You need to look for the campus energy that matches your own.

However, always be open to compromise. Your parents may have a differing opinion than you. If this is the case, you need to sit down with

200

them and discuss the opportunities and options.

Keep yourself from procrastinating. You have some real serious thinking to do. Make a list of the good things and the bad to help you make your decision. Bounce your thoughts off friends and family members. Be sure to submit whatever is required to secure your spot in the freshman class before the given deadline. The admissions offer letter from the school usually lists what the exact requirements are as to next steps.

If you have a tough time choosing among two or more schools, this is a positive sign. It means that you have done a good job putting together your list. Whichever institution you choose, chances are that you will be happy.

INTERNATIONAL COLLEGE COUNSELORS TIP: Be sure to make the most of your college experience. Chances are you'll never have the ability to return to a place with so many opportunities and so few responsibilities.

YOU ARE GOING TO COLLEGE!

Congratulations!

Once you have made your choice, accept it and rejoice. If you have followed the advice in this chapter, there is an excellent chance your final college choice is the right one for you.

We wish you great success in your academic endeavors and hope you enjoy your college studies. Remember, the college is accepting you— as a student, not as a school. Regardless of going to a public high school, with the right credentials and right application you, too, can get into an Ivy League school!

Chapter 25:
Calendars

At most public high schools, college guidance does not begin until junior year. And while this is "normal" and keeps college stress to a minimum, for those looking to attend an Ivy-level school, I recommend students start to think about college goals as early as 9th grade.

Below is a year-by-year checklist that will help keep you on track and avoid any last minute scramble.

HIGH SCHOOL FRESHMAN

Time Management

- Review your schedule at the beginning of the school year. The goal is to enroll in the most challenging classes you can handle.

- If possible, try to meet with a school counselor to discuss college plans. If you are considering hiring an independent counselor, make sure to find one who will begin your freshman year and has experience working with Ivy-level students.

- Don't procrastinate.

- Keep a calendar. Update it regularly with any important dates and deadlines.

Standardized Tests

Familiarize yourself with the SAT Subject Tests. Take the tests as soon as you finish the higher-level courses your school offers (usually AP) so the material is still fresh. While taking the highest-level course your school offers is rarely the case for freshman, it can happen. Subject Tests for freshman may include World History, Biology E/M, and Chemistry.

Read! It's the best way to prepare for the SAT and all standardized exams.

Extracurricular Activities

Get involved with extracurricular activities. Find something you know you enjoy or have interest in. This way, chances are you'll stick with it over the next four years. Colleges like to see that you stay with something and move up in it. Cooking, choir, Key Club, student government, racquetball, ceramics, speech and debate, or starting a business. It's all good. Many extracurricular activities show initiative, organizational skills, critical thinking, imagination, creativity, responsibility, commitment, and teamwork. Explore interests outside the school as well.

Key Projects or Involvement

Want to create something meaningful that will stand out for your applications? Whether you're starting a mentorship program, public safety campaign, new program or class, non-profit, or business venture, freshman year is a great time to get started.

Money

Talk with your parents about financing college. Talking about money will help you understand how much college really costs, and how you can help defray the costs through applying for private scholarships, taking AP courses, and getting good grades.

Learning Disabilities

If you think you have a learning disability, be sure to get tested as soon as possible. Most public schools offer free testing, although there may be a wait. You'll want to start getting the accommodations you may need to succeed.

Summer

If you're aiming for a top college, it's never too early to start with meaningful summer opportunities. Do some networking, and ask your parents and friends' parents to help you network, too. If you're interested in accounting, see who is in your network that you might be able to call. The same goes for if you want to be a graphic designer or a vet. Many businesses wouldn't mind a free volunteer.

Search online for summer programs for high school students at colleges, if this is the route you choose. Remember there is no "right" way to spend a summer—and you get no extra points for attending expensive, faraway programs. The trick is to engage in activities that are meaningful to you and provide opportunities for personal growth.

Learning about Colleges

Start to explore college websites and talk to older friends about colleges they're attending. Visit college campuses if you can. At this point in the game, it's low pressure. Make it fun. On a family vacation, make it a point to visit college campuses around your destination. Even if the schools are not on your radar, these visits will give everyone a chance to get a feel for the options.

HIGH SCHOOL SOPHOMORE

Time Management

- Review your schedule at the beginning of the school year. Continue to revise your academic program. The goal is to enroll in challenging classes that will help you prepare for college without overwhelming you.

- Keep up with your calendar. Update it regularly with any important dates and deadlines.

Standardized Tests

- Do not miss the PSAT/NMSQT, which is given in October. Most public schools offer this to their students starting in the 10th grade. Take this test for practice.

- If relevant, register for SAT II Subject tests in May or June and take SAT II and AP Tests as appropriate.

- Keep reading!

Extracurricular Activities

Stay involved in extracurricular activities. It's not too late to try new activities if you don't like the ones you participated in last year. Find something you know you enjoy or have interest in.

Revisit key activities and see how you can expand on your interests and abilities. Like volleyball? Consider starting a volleyball program for low-income students. Find that you are good at business? Enter national business plan competitions. Now is the time to start differentiating yourself, something that will be critical in Ivy-level admissions.

Money

Keep talking with your parents about financing college. How much are they able and willing to contribute to your education? Has their financial situation changed since your last conversation?

Surf the Internet for scholarship opportunities for sophomores. Apply to as many scholarships as possible. Make sure to meet all deadlines.

Summer

- Plan to do something exciting and explore a major interest. Interested in science or math? Consider one of the many competitive science/math summer programs, such as MIT's Research Science Institute (RSI) or Boston University's Program in Mathematics for

- Start visiting a few colleges.

- Use the summer to study for the SAT or ACT.

HIGH SCHOOL JUNIOR

Junior year is the homestretch. The critical decisions that are made this year could have a major impact on the next five years of your life— and long beyond. This is the year students start narrowing their lists of colleges and potential academic paths. This is the last full year of grades that college admissions officers will review.

Don't let the college admissions process feel so overwhelming you become frozen, missing deadlines and forgetting important details. Read this book and follow it and you'll be fine.

Time Management

- Review your schedule at the beginning of the school year. You want to enroll in challenging classes that will help you prepare for college. If you are aiming for the most competitive schools, you must take the most rigorous curriculum offered by your school. Care must be taken not to overload on classes or extracurricular activities, as junior-year courses and grades are critical. But, you need to show the college admissions team that you push yourself. Academically, this rule about focusing on grades and curriculum is relevant at all colleges—from the Ivy League to the less competitive.

- If you have not already done so, get to know your college counselor. He or she will likely be writing a letter of recommendation on your behalf. They can also make you aware of key scholarships and school awards.

- For those working with an independent counselor, set up a schedule for working together. This is an important year for support.

- Keep a calendar. Update it regularly with any important dates and deadlines.

Standardized Tests

- Make sure you take the PSAT/NMSQT, which is given in October. If you do well on the exam, you can qualify for a National Merit Scholarship.

- As quickly as possible, plan your junior year testing schedule. You can take either the SAT or up to three SAT Subject Tests on one test day, or the ACT, which is offered on other dates. You should aim to take the SAT and the ACT tests before the end of your junior year. We always recommend that students try BOTH the SAT and the ACT. The colleges (Ivies included) accept them equally, and students often have a natural inclination towards one test.

206

Extracurricular Activities

Colleges want to see that a student sticks with something. Remain involved with extracurricular activities. This year is very important. If you can, assume leadership roles in extracurricular activities. Now is the year to showcase your abilities at regional, state, or national competitions. Colleges aren't looking for quantity in activities, but quality. And advancement. This is your last year for colleges to understand your strength in debate, robotics, or art (to name a few). Don't be ashamed to seek opportunities to compete and shine.

Similarly, service activities should receive focus this year. Remember, the key to service is for the activity to be meaningful and impactful. It's not about how much money you raise or how far you travel to perform service. Some of the best service activities can be found in your own city and require little more than dedication, time, and creativity.

College Selection/Application Preparation

- Get to know the junior year teachers—and leave a positive impression on them. This is preparation for the all-important college recommendations.

- Start narrowing down colleges and universities. Information can be gathered in books and on websites. Try to talk to alumni or current students. In the spring, draft an initial college list. Before the start of senior year, the goal is to develop a list of fifteen to twenty colleges of interest.

- Talk about career choice(s). These may have a big impact on the list of potential colleges to be considered. The idea here is not to commit to a career path, but to try and narrow down the career possibilities.

- Go on college campus tours, as many as possible. Try to look at the whole range of schools: public, private, large, and small. Consider taking a college road tour over spring break.

- Attend any college fairs that come to your area, as well as presentations by traveling college admissions officers.

Money

▸ Keep talking with your parents about financing college. Make sure your parents' financial situation or amount they can contribute has not changed since your previous conversation.

▸ Research scholarship opportunities for juniors and apply to them. Make sure to proofread everything and meet all deadlines.

Summer

▸ Find a meaningful summer opportunity. This could include an internship, job, or college program. Whatever it is, start early. You want to beat the competition.

▸ This is the year when many competitive and prestigious summer programs are available. Interested in engineering? Journalism? Business? Consider filling out a few applications for programs that will help you learn and also look great on your college applications. Also consider summer programs at a college of interest. While this does not guarantee admissions, it will help you to confirm interest in the school and may make your early decision choice easier.

▸ Start to work on college applications! Schools with rolling admissions will accept applications as early as August or September, and early applications could mean early acceptances! For those schools not accepting applications until November or January, I still recommend that you complete your applications and essays as in the summer. There are no downsides to starting early. And it will save you significant time in the always-busy fall months.

▸ If you plan to retake your SAT or ACT in the fall, study as much as you can. This is your last chance!

All Year Round
Read! It's the best way to prepare for the SAT and all standardized exams.

HIGH SCHOOL SENIOR

For seniors, we've broken the "to-do" list down by months since there is a lot more to do.

August/September

- Confirm your college target list, and consider Early Action, Early Decision, and rolling admission possibilities.

- Plan to retake your SAT or ACT, as needed.

- Continue working on key target applications.

- Assign your recommenders/get your recommendation forms to your teachers and counselor early.

- Discuss with your high school counselor the colleges to which you are going to apply, and establish deadlines for the mailing of your transcripts.

October

- Do well academically—strong grades can have a major impact for regular admissions and if you are deferred from Early Decision.

- Complete Early Decision applications. Don't forget to send your test scores, transcripts, and any letters of recommendation.

- Get all necessary financial aid forms and explore scholarship opportunities.

- Check web portals/email for communication from colleges.

November

- Early Decision/Action candidates should be sure not to miss the application deadline this month.

- Arrange interviews with alumni and admissions representatives of colleges where interviews are available over the next several months.

- Send updates to schools you applied to early. Include in those updates any new activities or awards received since application submission.

▸ Check web portals/email for communication from colleges.

December

▸ This is likely your last chance to take your ACT, SAT, and SAT Subject Tests for fall admissions.

▸ If not on the Common Application, give your counselor, principal, or designated school official the secondary school report section of your college application forms early this month.

▸ If you have not done so already, give recommendation links/forms for each college to appropriate teachers and others. Let the teachers/counselors know if the Common Application will be emailing them directly.

▸ Be sure to continue working with your parents on appropriate financial aid forms.

▸ Early Decision applicants who have been admitted must withdraw any other applications.

▸ Early Decision applicants who have been deferred or rejected and non-Early Decision Round I applicants should consider Early Decision Round II opportunities at their first-choice school, if they have one and are ready to make a binding commitment.

▸ Preferably, all applications should be completed and sent out prior to holiday vacation.

January

▸ Applications for admission and financial aid forms must be mailed out or filed electronically to meet deadlines. Make copies of everything and check all details before submitting.

▸ Make sure recommendations and transcripts are being mailed/emailed.

▸ If you have been deferred from an early decision or early action school, do not dismay! Start writing a letter to the admission office bringing them up to date on your classes, activities, and continuing interest in the college. Send in any new materials or information worthy of inclusion in your application, for example, an additional recommendation from a senior-year teacher or new grades.

▸ Don't forget to keep up those grades. Good grades in the winter and spring can make a significant difference for deferred applications, regular applications, and, perhaps, a waiting list situation in May/June.

▸ Check web portals/email for communication from colleges.

February

▸ Arrange now to take AP tests in May or June. They could save you time and money in college!

▸ This is a good month to do self-marketing with faculty members and coaches at colleges.

▸ Send updates to early schools, including new awards, honors, or accomplishments received since the application was submitted.

▸ Finish all college applications.

▸ Take advantage of any alumni interviews that a college may offer you.

March

▸ Nail down sources of financial aid. Don't forget to apply for scholarships!

▸ Continue to work hard academically, and keep colleges informed of your progress, extracurricular achievements, and other awards.

▸ Check web portals/email for communication from colleges.

April

► This month you will receive your letters of admission.

► Check web portals/email for communication from colleges.

► Visit one or more campuses if necessary to help decide what college to accept.

► Make sure you are getting the best possible financial aid package, and let the financial aid office know of any dissatisfaction or questions you have. Aid packages can be revised.

► If you still want to attend a college that has wait-listed you, let the admissions office know your desire—send admissions officers any news, such as high grades or awards.

► Don't forget deposit deadlines.

► Check web portals/email for communication from colleges.

May

► Notification of acceptance deadline is May 1, known as the common reply date. You should also notify colleges you regretfully do not plan to attend, thanking them for accepting you.

► Take AP examinations.

► Take SAT II Subject Test as appropriate. This MAY help you gain extra credits and advanced course placement in college. (Check with your school.)

June

► Respond promptly to all requests from your college regarding housing preferences and preliminary selection of courses for first semester.

► Notify your high school to which college it should send your final grades, class rank, and proof of graduation.

► Plan to earn money this summer, or to get a head start on courses you will be taking.

▶ Make plans for any pre-orientation or freshman trip programs at the college.

▶ Drop a note of appreciation to your high school counselor, teachers, and any others who have helped you in the admission process.

▶ Celebrate your High School Success!